EVERYDAY
BULLETIN BOARDS

**for display throughout
the entire year**

EVERYDAY
BULLETIN BOARDS

By:

Liz Wilmes
&
Vohny Moehling

Art:

Nel Webster

A BUILDING BLOCKS Publication

38W567 Brindlewood, Elgin, Illinois 60123

COVER CONSULTANTS:
   Pat and Greg Samata
   Samata Associates, Inc.
   Dundee, Illinois 60118

PUBLISHED BY:
   BUILDING BLOCKS
   38W567 Brindlewood
   Elgin, Illinois 60123

DISTRIBUTED BY:
   GRYPHON HOUSE, Inc.
   P.O. Box 275
   Mt. Rainier, Maryland 20712

ISBN 0-943452-09-0
$8.95

Dedicated to:

. . . those who look at their bulletin boards in new and creative ways.

CONTENTS

MONTHLY MURALS (A Baker's Dozen)   Page

BORDER ACCENTS

"GETTING STARTED"

BORDER ACCENTS FRAME THE CHILDREN'S WORK, HIGHLIGHT AN ASPECT OF THE BOARD, TIE THE THEME OF THE BOARD TOGETHER, OR SIGNAL WHAT IS TO COME AS THE MAIN IDEA OF THE BOARD DEVELOPS. CHILDREN CAN EVEN BE INVOLVED ON TEACHER-MADE-BOARDS WHEN THEY CREATE THE BORDER ACCENTS.

CHILDREN CAN ALSO MAKE BORDERS FROM 'BEAUTIFUL JUNK' THAT THEY HAVE BROUGHT FROM HOME. (SEE APPENDIX FOR SUGGESTIONS.)

WHEN MAKING BORDERS:

- ENCOURAGE ALL OF THE CHILDREN TO GET INVOLVED.
- LET THE CHILDREN HELP YOU PREPARE SOME OF THE MATERIALS.
- ASK FOR VOLUNTEERS TO TALK WITH THE CHILDREN AS THEY MAKE THE BORDERS.
- HAVE THE CHILDREN HELP HANG THE BORDERS AROUND THE EDGES OF THE BULLETIN BOARD.
- CHANGE THE BORDERS AS OFTEN AS YOU LIKE.

FALL BORDERS

FALL ZIGZAGS

Materials:
Roll of mailing paper
Fall colored markers or crayons

Activity: Cut a piece of mailing paper the length of the longest side of your bulletin board. Lay it on the floor and let the children use markers or crayons to draw zigzag lines all over it.

Have the children help you cut the paper into appropriate width border strips and then tack them around the edges of your bulletin board. If you have children with more advanced cutting skills, you might ask them to cut a zigzag pattern rather than a straight line.

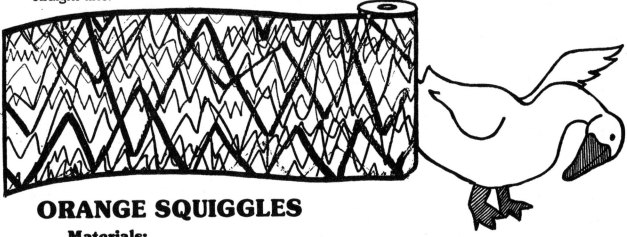

ORANGE SQUIGGLES

Materials:
Newspaper (no cartoons)
Heavy-duty string
Orange paint (equal parts liquid starch and liquid tempera) poured into
    shallow containers.

Activity: Open the paper and lay it on the floor. Let the children string-paint orange designs on it. When finished painting, leave the strings on the paper and they will stick.

When the paint is thoroughly dry, have the children help you cut the newspaper into strips to fit around the edges of the bulletin board. You can cut a straight edge or maybe a scalloped one.

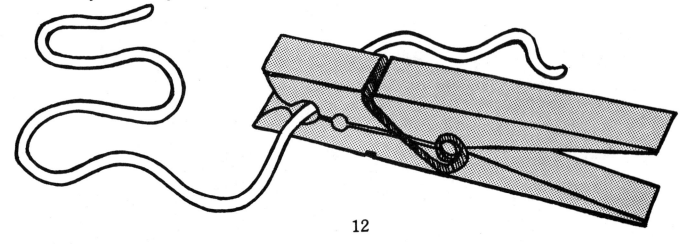

PAPER PUMPKINS

Materials:
Newspaper
Lunch-size bags
Twine
Orange and black tempera paint

Activity: Have the children scrunch-up newspaper and stuff the wads into lunch bags. Twist the tops and tie the bags closed with twine. Have the children paint their bags with orange paint. After the bags have dried hang them around the edges of your bulletin board.

Closer to Halloween the children might like to take their pumpkins down, paint jack-o-lantern faces on them, and re-hang them around the edges of the board.

POPCORN TRIM

Materials:
Orange posterboard
Glue
Different colors of popcorn kernels
Popped popcorn

Activity: Cut the posterboard into 3 inch wide strips. Put the strips, glue, and popcorn on the art table. Have the children glue the different types of popcorn to the strips. After the strips have dried, staple them around the bulletin board.

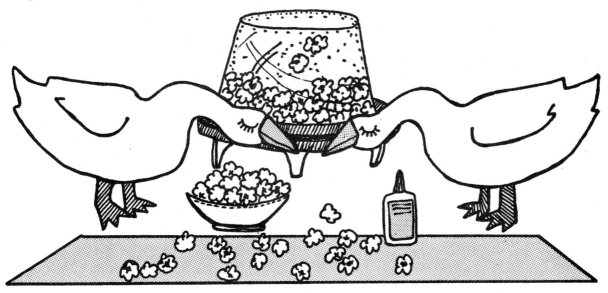

WINTER BORDERS

FOIL DRIZZLE

Materials:
Foil wallpaper
Glue in squeeze bottles
Glitter in shaker bottles

Activity: Cut the wallpaper into 3 inch wide strips. Put the strips on the art table along with the glue and glitter. Have the children drizzle glue on the strips and then sprinkle glitter over the glue. After the strips have dried, staple them around the bulletin board.

WHITE SHADOWS

Materials:
Red posterboard
Small paper doilies
White shoe polish in sponge
   applicator bottles

Activity: Lay several pieces of posterboard on the art table. Have the children lay doilies on the posterboard and paint over them with the sponge applicators. Carefully lift up the doilies and paint again in other spots. Continue until the posterboard has been completely stenciled. Let the paint dry, cut the board into strips, and then hang them up.

PILES OF SNOW

Materials:
Green posterboard
Styrofoam pieces
Glue

Activity: Cut the green posterboard into 3 inch wide strips. Have the strips, styrofoam pieces, and glue on the table. Let the children glue the pieces to the strips. Let the strips dry and then tack them around the edges of the board.

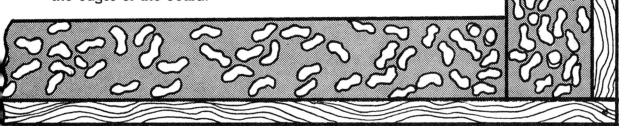

HEARTS AND FLOWERS

Materials:
Several small apples
Cauliflower pieces
Pink construction paper
Red and white tempera paint in meat trays

Activity: Cut each apple vertically in half to form two heart shapes and each cauliflower piece vertically in half to form the flower shapes. Put a fork in each apple and cauliflower piece for a handle. Cut the paper into strips about 3 inches wide. Or mark the paper and let the children cut their own strips.

Pour the paint into meat trays. Have the children dip the fruit and vegetable stamps into the paint and press the shapes onto the strips. Continue dipping and pressing until the strips are full of 'hearts and flowers'. Let the strips dry and then hang.

SPRING BORDERS

SPRING WIND

Materials:
Newspaper
Heavy-duty paper such as construction paper
Bright colors of florescent tempera paint
Teaspoons
Straws

Activity: Have the children lay pieces of construction paper on the newspaper, pour small spoonfuls of paint on the construction paper, and then blow the paint around through the straws. Add more paint if they want and continue blowing. Let the construction paper dry.

Draw lines on the paper for the children to follow as they cut the paper into border strips. Hang them around the bulletin board. Add kites to each corner if you want.

SWISS CHEESE

Materials:
Regular or wide adding machine tape
Paper punches
Meat trays

Activity: Roll out a part of the tape and have the children punch holes all along it. Save the 'confetti' on meat trays for another activity. Continue until the children have punched enough tape to go around the bulletin board. Hang it. If you have a large bulletin board you may want to have a double border.

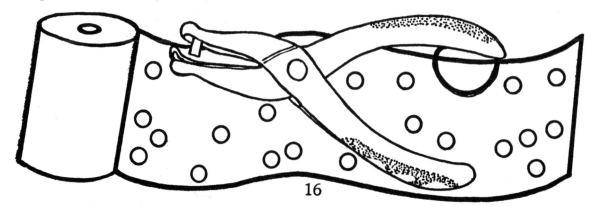

RAIN-DROP CHAINS

Materials:
Spring-colored construction paper
Large meat trays
Glue or paste

Activity: Have the children cut strips of construction paper and put them on the meat trays. Help each child get started by having him dab glue onto one end of a strip, join the other tip so that the two ends are 'kissing' and hold them together until they are dry. Then he can loop another strip through the first one, dab glue on one tip, 'kiss' the ends, and hold them until dry. Each child can continue linking his own chain for as long as he wants.

When everyone has finished his chain, have the children help you link all of the individual chains together to make one long enough to go around the board.

POLKA DOT TRIM

Materials:
White or pastel colored posterboard
Different sizes, designs, and colors of dot-type stickers

Activity: Cut the posterboard into 2 or 3 inch wide strips to go around the edges of the bulletin board. Have the children put the various dots on all of the strips and then tack them to the board.

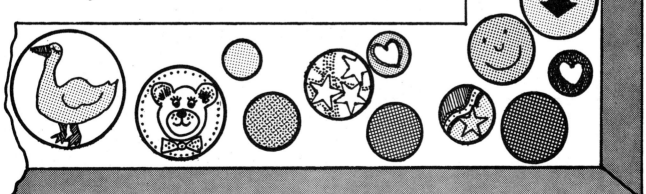

SUMMER BORDERS

RAINBOW SWIRLS

Materials:
Crayon stubs
Aluminum foil muffin cups
White shelf paper

Activity: First have the children help you make cookie crayons. They should tear all of the paper off of the crayons and put the stubs in muffin cups. Put the cups out in the sun. Let the crayons melt and then harden there overnight. The next morning tear the muffin cups away from the crayons.

Lay the shelf paper on the floor or table. Have the children draw rainbow swirls all over the paper with their new crayons. When finished, cut the paper into appropriate widths to trim your bulletin board.

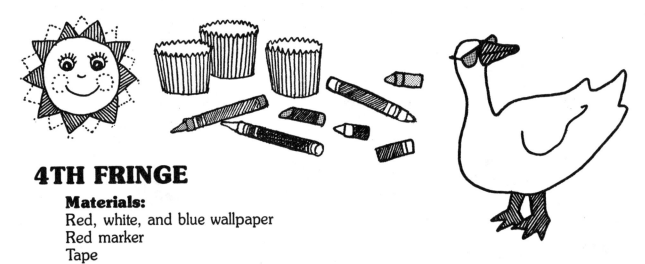

4TH FRINGE

Materials:
Red, white, and blue wallpaper
Red marker
Tape
Scissor

Activity: Cut the wallpaper into 3 inch wide strips. On the backside of the strips, about 1 inch from one of the horizontal edges draw "STOP" lines with a wide marker. Tape the strips low on a wall or onto your art table.

Have the children snip the paper trying to stop near the marked line. When finished carefully take each strip off of the wall or table, wrap the tape over the top of the strip to give it added strength and then hang the fringed strips around the bulletin board.

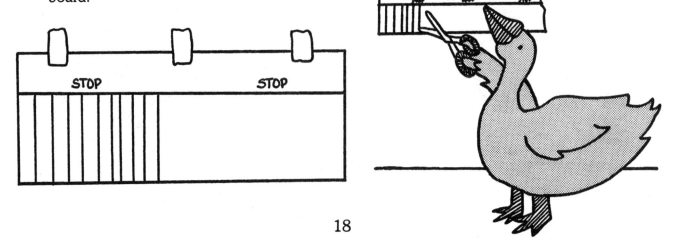

BRIGHT CIRCLES

Materials:
Small white paper plates
Florescent paint

Activity: Have the children paint the plates. Let them dry and then staple them to the edges of the board. For extra shine add a little salt to the paint.

ICE CREAM CONES

Materials:
Variety of wallpaper including
    a light brown textured piece
Scissors

Activity: Cut 2 cones out of the piece of brown textured wallpaper. From the other pieces of wallpaper have the children choose pieces that represent flavors of ice cream which they like and then cut out as many scoops as they want. They can help you tack the scoops to the border.

19

BACKGROUND BRIGHTENERS

"GETTING STARTED"

BACKGROUND BRIGHTENERS ARE LARGE, EASY, CHILD-MADE CREATIONS. THEY CAN STAND ALONE OR ACT AS BACKDROPS FOR OTHER ACTIVITIES THE CHILDREN HAVE BEEN INVOLVED IN OR CREATIONS THEY HAVE MADE. INCLUDED WITH EACH BACKGROUND BRIGHTENER IDEA IS AN 'EXTENSION' ACTIVITY WHICH COORDINATES WITH THE BACKGROUND.

IN ADDITION TO THE BACKGROUNDS WHICH THE CHILDREN CREATE, THEY MAY WANT TO BRING ITEMS FROM HOME TO PUT ON THE BOARD FOR BACKGROUNDS. (SEE APPENDIX FOR SUGGESTIONS.)

WHEN PLANNING THE BACKGROUND BRIGHTENER IDEAS REMEMBER:

- GATHER ALL OF THE MATERIALS AHEAD OF TIME.
- SET UP THE ACTIVITY IN AN AREA WHERE THE CHILDREN CAN EASILY WORK ON IT.
- USE THE EXTENSION IDEAS IF YOU HAVE A LARGE BULLETIN BOARD.
- USE THE EXTENSION IDEAS AS PRESENTED OR VARY THEM FOR YOUR GROUP OF CHILDREN.

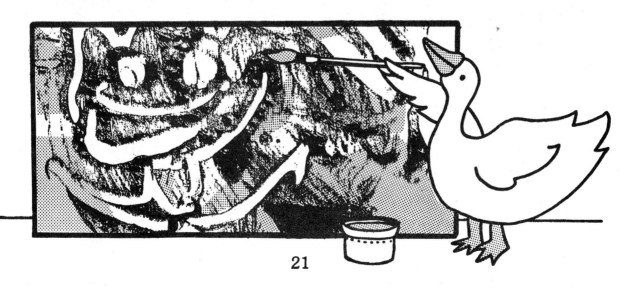

21

ROLLER-COASTER

Materials:
Butcher paper the size of your bulletin board
All different lengths, widths, and colors of construction paper strips
Paste

Activity: Tape the butcher paper to your art table or floor. Put the paper strips in several containers and place them around the butcher paper.

Have the children paste the strips on the butcher paper in all different ways. The children might paste the strips flat, make tall mountains or bridges, curve or twist them, and so on. You could also encourage the children to loop the strips over each other.

After all of the children have finished, hang the roller-coaster on the bulletin board.

EXTENSION: Take photographs of the children building their roller-coaster. After the photos are developed, hang them on and between the different curves and bumps.

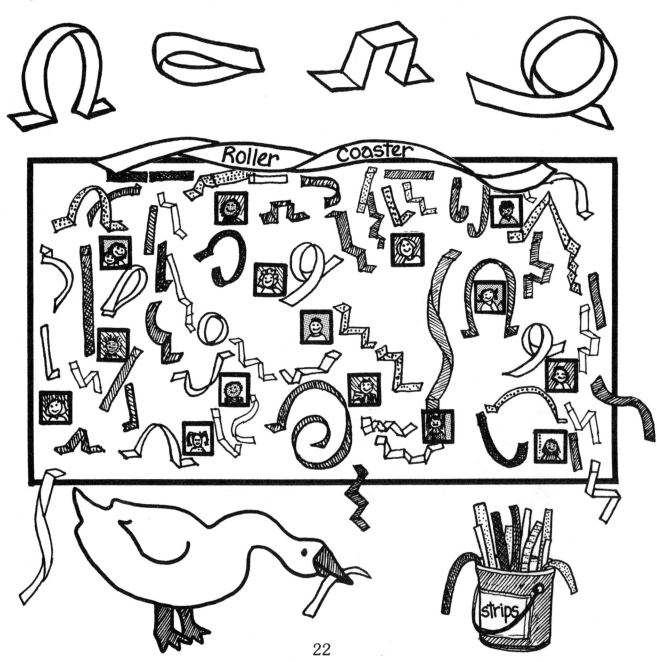

CRAZY QUILT

Materials:
Construction paper squares
Smooth wood pieces or small wooden objects in different shapes and sizes
4 or 5 colors of tempera paint in shallow containers

Activity: Let each child pick his favorite color of paint and several pieces of wood. Using the wooden shapes have him print on a piece of construction paper. Encourage the children to pick other colors and enjoy printing more wood designs. Let the quilt squares dry and then arrange and tack them to the bulletin board to make the Crazy Quilt.
EXTENSION: Have the children make paper bag puppets and tuck the puppets into the quilt as if they are napping.

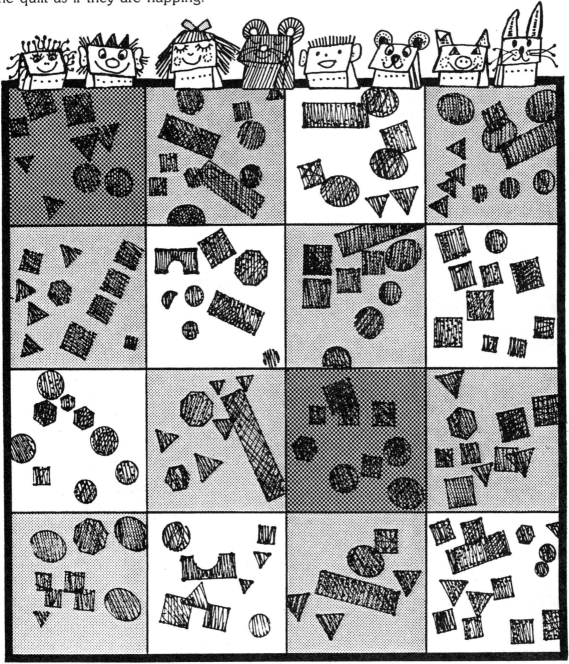

FEATHER PAINTING

Materials:
Butcher paper the size of your bulletin board
Variety of colors of tempera paint in large containers
Feather duster for each container of paint

Activity: Tape the butcher paper to the floor or art table. Use the dusters as brushes. Encourage the children to paint the butcher paper all different colors. As the children are painting they can pretend that the feathers on the dusters are turkey feathers and talk to each other in turkey language such as "Gobble, gobble, gobble." When dry, hang up the Feather Painting.
EXTENSION: When the Feather Painting is dry and before you hang it up, have the children add a flock of hand print turkeys to the field. The children can add details to their turkeys with fine-tipped markers.

24

WRAPPING UP

Materials:
Freezer wrap paper to cover your bulletin board
Bright colored wallpaper or heavy wrapping paper
Large paper plate or posterboard circle

Activity: Cover the board with freezer wrap paper, shiny side facing out. Cut the colored paper into two different strips: one strip should be about 5 inches wide and the height of your board; the other one should be about 5 inches wide and the width of your board. Attach the two strips on the board to form a ribbon on the package.

Using the same colored paper, cut strips about 12″ × 1-1/2″. Have the children form the bow for the ribbon by making individual raindrop links, giving each link to you, and letting you arrange and staple them onto the paper plate to form a giant looped bow. Tack the bow to the center of the ribbon.
EXTENSION: Use the 4 sections of the package to display 4 different holiday art activities.

IT'S SNOWING

Materials:
Light blue paper the size of your bulletin board
Toilet paper rolls
Scissors
White tempera paint mixed with a little Ivory Snow® poured into large shallow
  containers

Activity: Tape the paper to the floor. Have the children cut each of the toilet
paper rolls lengthwise into 4 to 6 strips no more than 2/3 of the way up the roll.
Bend each of the strips back.

Put the containers of textured paint around the paper. Have the children
press their cut toilet paper rolls into the paint and print several snowflakes on the
butcher paper. Re-press or use other rolls and print more snowflakes. Continue for
as long as the children would like. Let the paper dry and then hang it up.
EXTENSION: Have the children make different types of snowflakes by cutting
doilies into different shapes, folding coffee filters or paper muffin cup liners in half
and cutting designs along the folded edges, cutting designs into white paper, and
so on. Hang them on the board.
EXTENSION: Use the snow scene as a background for snowpeople.

HEART HUNT

Materials:
Butcher paper the size of your bulletin board
Many different size posterboard heart shapes
Double-stick tape
Different colors of chalk
Fixative for the chalk

Activity: Using double-stick tape, stick the heart shapes all over the art table. Lay the butcher paper over the shapes and tape it to the table. Have chalk in containers.

Show the children how to hunt for the hearts by rubbing their hands over the paper. As they find hearts have them use the side of the chalk and make rubbings. After they have made all of their heart rubbings, spray the mural with a fixative so the chalk does not smear. Hang.

EXTENSION: Attach Valentines that the children have created.

EXTENSION: Remove all of the posterboard hearts from the art table and tape them over the rubbings. Hang.

TEMPERA SWIRLS

Materials:
Brown mailing paper the size of your bulletin board
Tempera paint in roller bottles

Activity: Tape the mailing paper to the floor. Using the roller bottles have the children paint the paper. Encourage the children to experiment with the roller bottles as they paint. They might want to hold the bottle in one hand and then the other. They could swirl it, curve it, go slow and fast, make short lines and long ones.
When finished hang it on the board. Talk about all of the colors and lines.

EXTENSION: After the tempera swirls have dried put a variety of colors and weights of yarn along with glue on the table. Have the children glue the yarn along some of the paint lines. When finished hang it on the board.

EYE-DROPPER RAIN

Materials:
Rolls of heavy-duty paper towels
Different colors of food coloring mixed with a little water
Plastic eyedroppers

Activity: Lay several paper towel strips on the art table. Put the bowls of colored water and the eyedroppers around the toweling. Have the children drop dots of colored water onto the strips. Let the strips thoroughly dry and then staple them to the bulletin board.
EXTENSION: Have the children make ocean creatures to swim amongst the colorful bubbles.

29

ART GALLERY

Materials:
Butcher paper the size of your bulletin board
Small paint-trimming rollers
Pastel colored tempera paint in meat trays
Variety of children's art

Activity: Tape the butcher paper to the floor or art table. Put the paint rollers and tempera paint around the edges of the paper. Have the children dip the rollers into the paint and make pastel tracks over the entire paper. Let it dry and hang it on the bulletin board.
EXTENSION: Each day during the month have a different child choose which piece of his art he wants to display in the Art Gallery. Help him frame it. You can frame children's artwork in several ways:

• Cut strips of construction paper and glue them around the edges of the artwork.

• Water down white glue. Brush it on the back of the art. Mount the art on a doily, paper plate, piece of construction paper, wallpaper sample, paper placemat, or other type of paper.

After the artwork is framed, hang it in the Art Gallery.

WIGGLY WEAVING

Materials:

Fish net or a fish net hammock

Different types of weaving materials (fabric strips, clothesline, paper strips, heavy
   yarn and wide ribbon)

Heavy-duty tape

Activity: If you have a low bulletin board, attach the net to the board. If you do
not, tack the net low on the board and let it drape below the board so that the
children can easily weave the top section of the net. Have the weaving materials in a
container nearby. If the children are weaving with clothesline, yarn, ribbon, and/or
fabric strips, tie one end of the strips to the netting to make it easier for the children to
weave. After they have woven the top section of the net, move the net up and let the
children weave the bottom section. When finished, position the weaving and securely
tack it to the bulletin board.

EXTENSION: Using clothespins, hang the children's artwork from the weaving.

31

ARM DANCING

Materials:
Butcher paper the size of your bulletin board
Crayons
Several musical selections with different beats

Activity: Lay the butcher paper on the floor. Tape down the corners. Have the children sit all around the edges of the paper. Pass the crayons around and let each child pick two.

Tell the children to hold one crayon in each hand. Play some music so that they can listen and get the beat. Now play the music again and have them color the paper to the beat. After awhile stop the music. Play another selection and have the children color to the beat of that music.

When the paper is full of color, stop and talk about it. Hang it up.

EXTENSION: Before hanging up the children's Arm Dancing Mural, have them add more color to it by dipping plastic child-size garden tools in tempera paint and then pretending to rake, hoe, and shovel on the paper.

EXTENSION: Before hanging up the children's Arm Dancing Mural, have the children cut out magazine pictures of people using their arms in different ways and glue them onto the paper. Talk about what the arms are doing as the children are gluing.

CAR TRACKS

Materials:
Old road maps
Tempera paint in shallow containers
Several small cars and other vehicles

Activity: Tape several road maps to the art table. Pour the different colors of tempera paint into shallow containers. Let the children dip the vehicles into the paint and drive them over the maps as if the children were on a trip. Encourage them to re-dip their vehicles and continue their trip. When dry, tack the maps to the board. EXTENSION: Have the children dictate something about their trips or draw pictures of them. Hang the pictures and dictations around the edges of the board.

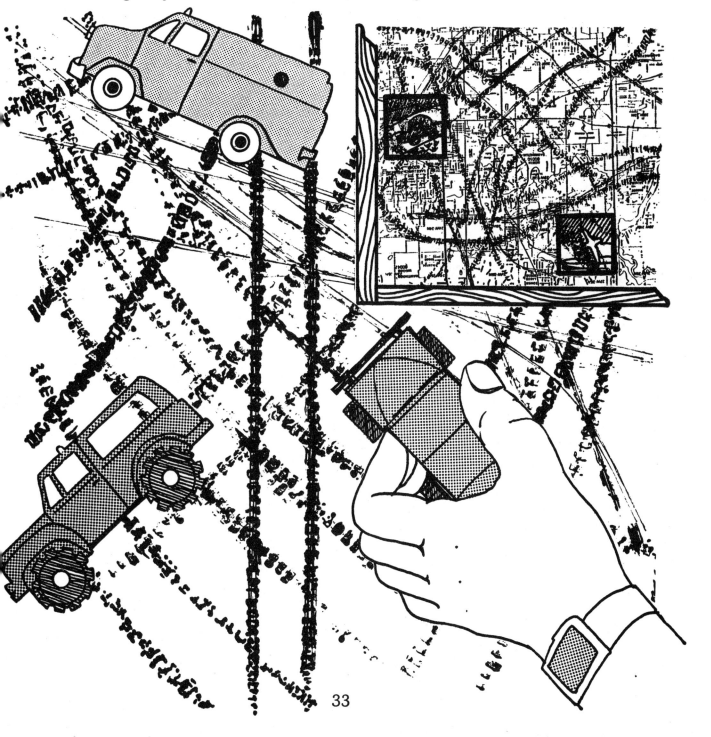

MONTHLY MURALS

"GETTING STARTED"

MONTHLY MURALS SPOTLIGHT SOMETHING SPECIAL ABOUT EACH MONTH OF THE YEAR. THEY HELP THE CHILDREN CELEBRATE HOLIDAYS AND SEASONS, RECOGNIZE CHANGING WEATHER CONDITIONS, AND HIGHLIGHT SPECIAL EVENTS.

AS THE CHILDREN ENJOY DOING EACH MURAL REMEMBER:

- TALK WITH THEM ABOUT THE MATERIALS THEY ARE USING.
- EXTEND THE MURAL ACTIVITY USING THEIR IDEAS.
- ADD BORDERS TO THE MURALS IF YOU WISH.
- TAKE YOUR TIME. THE CHILDREN MAY WANT TO TAKE SEVERAL DAYS TO COMPLETE THE MURAL.
- USE THE MURAL AS A FOCAL POINT FOR CLASSROOM DISCUSSIONS THROUGHOUT THE MONTH.
- ENCOURAGE THE CHILDREN TO HELP YOU TAKE THE MURAL DOWN AT THE END OF EACH MONTH. EACH CHILD MAY WANT TO TAKE A SECTION OF IT HOME.

WELCOME NEW FRIENDS

Materials:
Piece of light colored paper the size of your bulletin board
Toilet paper roll for each child
Several different colors of tempera paint poured into large containers such as
  brownie pans
Recent photo of each child

Activity: During the first week of school take a photograph of each child or have
each child bring a recent photo of himself to school.

Lay the paper on the floor. Place the other
supplies nearby. Have each child pick a toilet paper
roll and cut it lengthwise into 4 to 6 strips about
halfway up the roll. Bend the strips back a little. Then
have each child press the flared part of his roll into
one of the paints and make a print on the paper. Let
the paint dry and then have the child glue his photo in
the center of the design. Print each child's name by his
photo. When everyone has finished, hang the mural
on the board.

Maria

Christo

Jesse

Shannon

CELEBRATE FALL

Materials:
Gold paper or fabric the size of your bulletin board
Red, orange, purple, and brown tempera paint in shallow containers
Large sheet of paper the size of a child
White glue
Blue and orange tempera paint
Fabric and wallpaper scraps
Scissors or pinking shears
Straw (optional)

Activity: Tape the paper or fabric to the art table or floor. Put the paint containers around the paper. Have the children lay their hands in the paint and then press them firmly on the paper or fabric creating piles of fall-colored leaves. Encourage the children to try different colors. Let the mural dry and hang it on the bulletin board.

After the leaves have been up for several days have the children make a scarecrow. Lay the large sheet of paper on the floor. Have a child lie down on the paper, pretending to be a scarecrow, Trace around the child and cut out his shape. Hang the undressed scarecrow on the pile of colored leaves.

Add blue tempera paint to some of the glue and orange paint to the rest. Cut the fabric and wallpaper scraps into different size patches. Take the scarecrow off of the board and tape it to the art table.

Have the children brush glue onto the scarecrow shape, choose patches, lay them on the glue, and give each patch a pat to make sure it sticks. After all of the patches have been glued on, you might want to add straw to the scarecrow's feet, arms and wherever else you'd like. Tack your dressed scarecrow to the board amongest the piles of colored leaves.

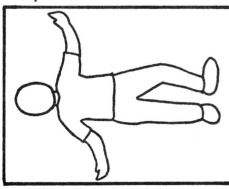

FALL WALK

Materials:
Butcher paper the size of your bulletin board
Lunch sacks
Nature items
Meat tray for each child

Activity: On a warm day give each child a sack and go for a fall walk. As you are walking have the children pick up nature items which interest them. When you return give each child a meat tray. Print his name on it. Have each child pour all of his items onto his tray.

Tape the piece of butcher paper to the floor. Let the children glue the items they found on the walk to the butcher paper. When each child is finished, print his name near his collection. Let it dry and then hang it up.

EXTENSION: Give each child the opportunity to dictate something about his collection. Write what he says on a lunch sack and tack it near his collection.

THANKSGIVING DINNER

Materials:
Old fabric tablecloth or a heavyweight paper tablecloth the approximate size of
   your bulletin board
Different colors of tempera paint poured into shallow meat trays
Different kitchen utensils for printing
Paper plates
Food magazines

Activity; Lay the tablecloth on the art table. Add the paint and utensils. Have the children stand around the table and make prints on the cloth with the different utensils and colors of paint. Let the cloth dry and hang it up.

Over the next several days have the children look through magazines, find their favorite Thanksgiving foods, tear or cut them out, and glue them onto paper plates. Have each child (or you) print his name on a name card and staple it to his plate. When everyone has finished preparing his Thanksgiving Dinner, set the table by hanging all of the plates on the tablecloth.

39

HOLIDAY GIFTS

Materials:
White butcher paper the size of your bulletin board
Bright colored tempera paint (Add liquid detergent to the paint so it adheres to
    the boxes which have a shiny surface)
Variety of holiday cookie cutters
All sizes and shapes of gift boxes
Colored confetti
Heavy-duty pins

Activity: Before beginning this bulletin board activity, talk with the children and
decide what short holiday message such as "HAPPY HOLIDAYS" they would like to
have on their board.
    Using the butcher paper, paint, and cookie cutters have the children print the
butcher paper. When it is dry, hang it up.
    Put the gift boxes on the table. Have the children paint them. When the boxes
have completely dried, use a marker to print one letter of the holiday message on each
box top. Have each child brush glue over his letter and sprinkle it with confetti. Let dry.
    Using heavy-duty straight pins tack the bottoms of the boxes in order onto the
board. Put the tops on, sending the holiday message to everyone. The children might
want to collage large candles or Santa stockings for each side of the message.

SNOWBALL FUN

Materials:
Butcher paper the size of your bulletin board
Different colors of powdered tempera paint in shaker containers
Small snowballs or ice cubes
Different size white posterboard circles ranging from small to very large depending
    on the size of your board
Different white materials, such as styrofoam, fabrics, yarn, papers, cotton, etc.
Doilies

Activity: Tape the butcher paper to the floor. Have the children sprinkle it with
dry tempera. Get a container full of snow. Put it near the butcher paper. Wearing
mittens, have the children make snowballs and glide them over the paper and through
the paint. Let the mural dry and then hang it up.

Have the children glue the white materials to the different size circles. You can do
this anyway the children would like. You might want to simply let them glue the white
materials randomly on the different snowballs or you might want to separate the
materials and have a soft snowball, a rough snowball, and a smooth snowball to
provide a wide variety of textures for your board. As each snowball is finished, tack it
to the brightly colored background paper.

Add snowflakes the children have cut out of doilies.

VALENTINE TELEGRAMS

Materials:
Valentine wrapping paper or butcher paper the size of your bulletin board
Glue in shallow containers
Small red, pink, and white tissue paper squares
Pencils with erasers
Special telegram paper

Activity: Lay the paper on the floor. Depending on the size of your bulletin board, draw one huge heart or several very large ones on the paper. Have the glue, tissue paper squares, and pencils on the floor.

Have a child take a piece of tissue paper, lay it in front of him, put the pencil eraser in the middle of the paper, and form the tissue around the pencil. Dip the tissue in the glue and stick it on the edge of the heart. Let all of the children continue this process until the heart has a frame. When dry hang it up.

For several days let the children dictate Valentine messages which you can write on the special telegram paper. When each message is finished hang it inside a giant heart.

EXTENSION: Return the telegrams to the children before Valentines Day and let them distribute their messages.

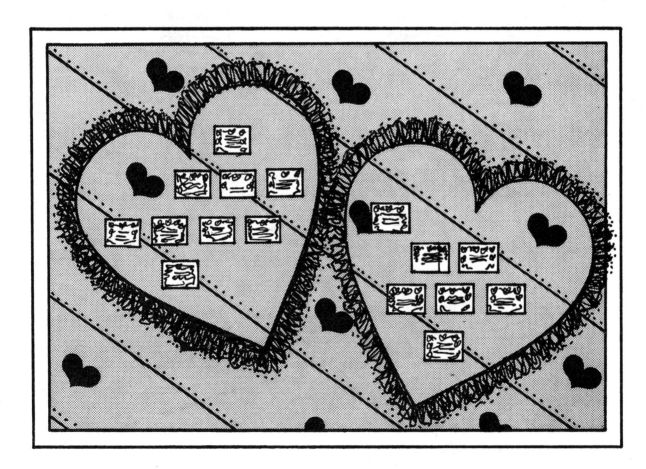

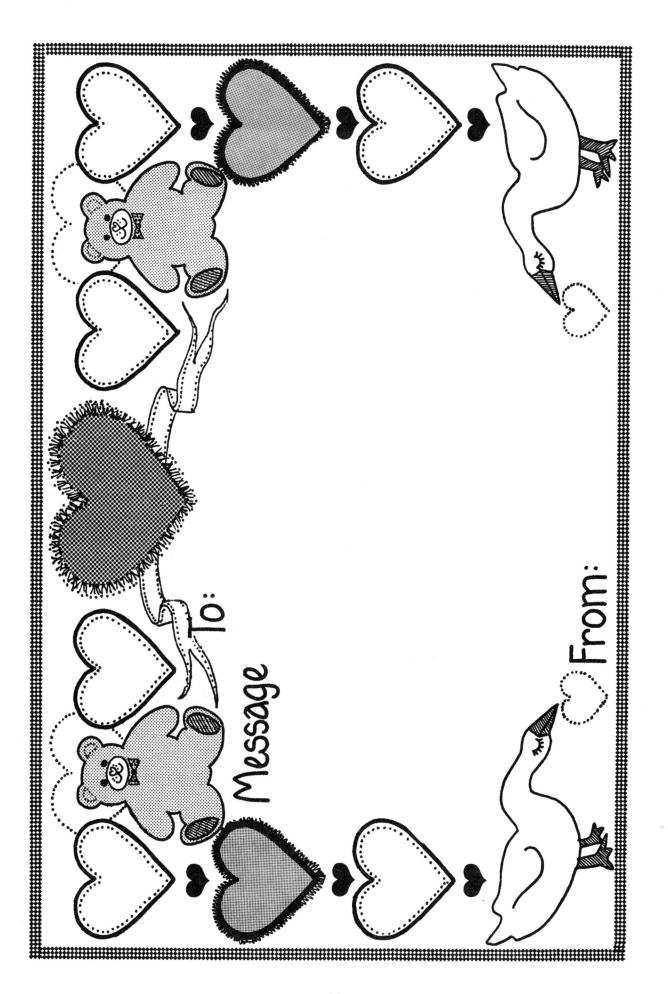

To:

Message

From:

UP, UP, AND AWAY

Materials:
Light blue butcher paper the size of your bulletin board
White tempera paint in pie pans
Sponges
Large piece of white butcher paper
Variety of colors of tissue paper torn into small pieces
Liquid starch in pie pans
Twine or yarn
Berry basket

Activity: Tape the light blue butcher paper to the art table. Have the children sponge paint white clouds on it. When it is dry, hang it on your bulletin board.

Cut the white butcher paper into a large hot air balloon shape that will fill most of your board. Lay newspaper on the floor. Put the balloon shape on the newspaper. Put the starch and tissue paper pieces near the balloon. Have the children put pieces of tissue paper on the balloon, dip their fingers into the starch and gently rub the starch over the tissue pieces to stick them down. Continue until the entire balloon is full of color.

Let the balloon dry and then attach it to the bulletin board to float amongst the clouds. Attach twine or yarn to the neck of the balloon and then tie a berry basket to the ends for the gondola.

44

SHOWING OFF

Materials:
Butcher paper the size of your bulletin board
3 types of paint, such as watercolors, fingerpaint, and tempera
3 types of paper such as coffee filters, freezer wrap, and wallpaper

Activity: Divide the butcher paper into thirds and hang. Label each section. On separate days let the children use 3 different paints. For example they could watercolor on large coffee filters, fingerpaint on freezer paper, and tempera paint on wallpaper. Let the artwork dry.

Give each child the choice of taking his art home or hanging it on the bulletin board. Hang all of the watercolor paintings in the first section, fingerpaint in the second section, and tempera in the third.
EXTENSION: Change the labels and repeat this activity using chalks in 3 different ways, 3 types of crayons, and/or 3 types of collage materials such as paper, fabric, and yarn.

SCHOOL'S SPECIAL

Materials:
Butcher paper the size of your bulletin board
Different colors of fingerpaint in large shallow containers
Wide-tipped marker
Container of water
Roll of paper towels

Activity: Lay the butcher paper on the floor. Have the marker and containers of fingerpaint nearby. During the time when the children are working independently, have them come over one at a time to make their hand and footprints on the butcher paper.

First have the child pick what color paint he wants his prints to be, take off his shoes and socks, step into the paint, and then onto the paper to make his footprints. Afterwards help him wash and dry his feet and have him put his shoes and socks back on. Then he should lay his hands in the fingerpaint and make his hand prints near his footprints. Have him wash and dry his hands.

Write the child's name and the date near the prints and have him dictate some of the things he really liked about school this year. Write his thoughts near the prints. Continue until you have given each child in your class the opportunity to make his prints and dictate favorite things about school. Let the prints dry and then hang the mural up.

EXTENSION: When you take the board down, cut each child's prints and dictation out and frame it by gluing it to a large piece of construction paper. Send it home as a momento of the school year.

Kristen
May 1988

46

SUMMER'S BUZZING

Materials:
Pastel colored butcher paper the size of your bulletin board
A small tree branch for each color of tempera paint
Bright colors of tempera paint in pie pan containers
Dark colors, (black, brown, purple) of fingerpaint in small containers
Fine-tipped markers

Activity: Tape the butcher paper to the floor or lay it on the ground outside. Put one branch in each paint container. Using the branches as brushes, have the children paint the paper. Let the paint dry.

Using the fingerpaint, let the children make thumb, fist, palm, and fingerprint insects all over the paper. The children may want to use the markers to add legs, antennae, and other details to their mosquitoes, ants, ladybugs, flies, etc. Hang up the display of summer insects.

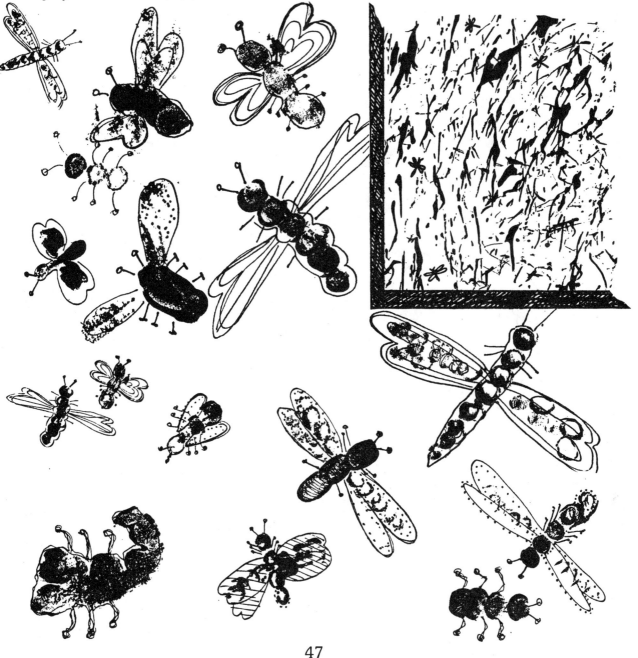

FIREWORKS TONIGHT

Materials:
Butcher paper the size of your bulletin board
Large adhesive dots
Glitter (all colors)
Glue
Star stickers

Activity: Lay the butcher paper on the floor. Put the dots on the paper to indicate the center of each firework. Have the children drizzle glue lines starting from the dots. Shake glitter along the lines creating a skyful of sparkling, glittering fireworks. After the glue has dried, shake off the excess glitter and then add the stars and a moon. Hang the fireworks display on the board.

BOAT FLOAT

Materials:
Yellow butcher paper for the bottom third of your bulletin board
Light blue butcher paper for the top two-thirds of your bulletin board
Wide brushes
Glue
Sand in shaker bottles
Sponges cut into designs
White tempera paint in pie pans
Small milk or whipping cream cartons
All colors of bright tempera paint. Add liquid detergent to each color so it
    adheres to the milk cartons better
Vinyl wallpaper
Straws

Activity: Tape the yellow butcher paper to the floor. Have the children brush glue on it and shake sand on the glue. Let it dry, carefully shake off the excess sand, and hang it on the board.

Tape the blue butcher paper to the floor. Have the children sponge paint clouds near the top of the paper. They might want to add a sun, airplanes, bugs, etc. When dry hang it up.

Let the children make colorful boats by painting the cartons different colors. If the children would like to make sailboats, have them cut the sails from wallpaper, stick a straw through each one and insert the sails into milk cartons. Let each child decide if his boat is sailing in the water or docking on the sand. Tack the boats to the board.
EXTENSION: When you take the board down, let the children float their boats in the water table.

SPECIAL SPACES

"GETTING STARTED"

SPECIAL SPACES PROVIDE EACH CHILD WITH HIS OWN SPOT TO DISPLAY HIS NEWEST TREASURES, SUCH AS ARTWORK, PHOTOGRAPHS, VACATION MEMORABILIA, AND MAGAZINE PICTURES. THESE ARE GREAT BOARDS FOR HELPING CHILDREN TO LEARN TO MAKE CHOICES.

WHEN USING ONE OF THE SPECIAL SPACES BULLETIN BOARDS REMEMBER:

- BACKGROUNDS STAY THE SAME.
- PATTERNS MAY BE ENLARGED OR REDUCED.
- CHILDREN CHOOSE WHAT THEY WANT TO DISPLAY ON THEIR SPACES.
- CHILDREN MAY CHOOSE TO HAVE THEIR SPACES EMPTY AT TIMES.
- CHILDREN SHOULD TAKE THEIR OLD MATERIAL HOME WHEN PUTTING UP THEIR NEW MATERIAL.
- CHILDREN CAN CHOOSE TO CHANGE THEIR TREASURES AS OFTEN AS THEY WANT.

FLAGPOLE DISPLAY

Materials:
Sky blue butcher paper to cover your board
Narrow dowel rods
Different colored construction paper (11"×14" works best on a large board.)
Wide tipped markers

Activity: Hang the butcher paper on the bulletin board. Glue the flag poles to the background being sure to leave enough space between poles to staple the children's flags next to them. (See illustration). Have the children decorate their flags with markers.

After each child finishes his flag, write his name on it. Ask him which pole he would like to fly his flag from. Tack it next to the pole he chooses. Now his flag is ready to display his art or other work on.

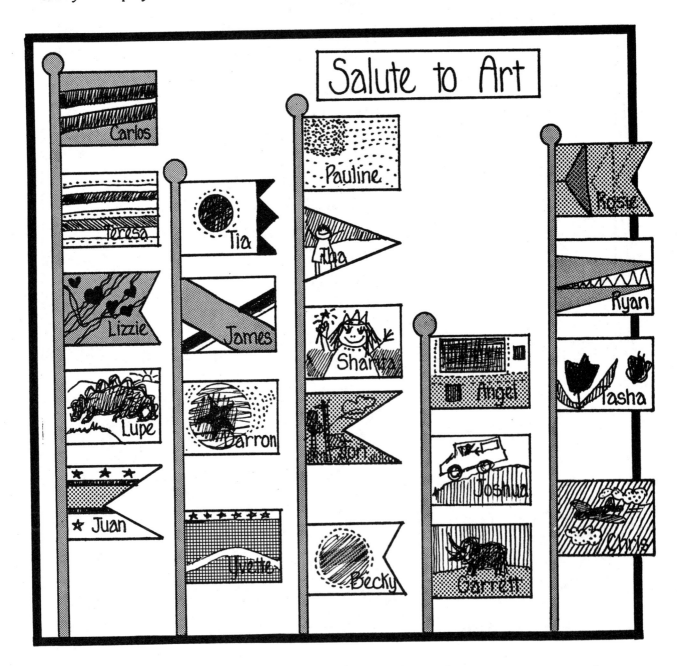

52

PERSONAL PAN ART

Materials:
Bright butcher paper or gift wrap to cover your bulletin board
12 inch pizza boards
Different art media with which to decorate the boards (markers, crayons, chalk, colored pencils, paint)
Heavy-duty straight pins

Activity: Hang the butcher paper on the bulletin board. Let each child decorate his pizza board with any of the art media available. After each child's board is dry, ask him where he would like you to write his name on it. Write it for him.

Have the children help you arrange their boards on the bulletin board. As you are hanging the decorated pizza boards remind each child which board is his. Talk about how each one looks. For example, "Juan, you painted your special space with all colors of paint. Look, here is red (point), here is some blue, and look, here is green at the bottom." Do this with each child's board to help him remember what his board looks like.

53

TRAIN CAR POCKETS

Materials:
Butcher paper to cover the bulletin board
Tagboard
All colors of tempera paint
Construction paper

Activity: Cover the bulletin board with the butcher paper. Cut out one engine, you paint it and tack it to the bulletin board. Cut out a large train car shape from tagboard for each child. Let him pick the car he would like and then paint it at the easel. Let it dry and then write his name on it.

After all of the train cars have dried have the children help you connect them into a train. Staple each car securely to the board on three sides, leaving the top side open. (These train cars may run off the board onto your walls.) As you're putting the cars up talk with the children about how each one was painted. When all of the cars are up, the children might want to make short paper chains and link the cars together. They might also want to cut tracks.

Each child can decide if he wants to display his work on the outside of his car, let the work peek over the top, or hide it inside especially if it has been made for someone.

On Track In The Sunshine Room

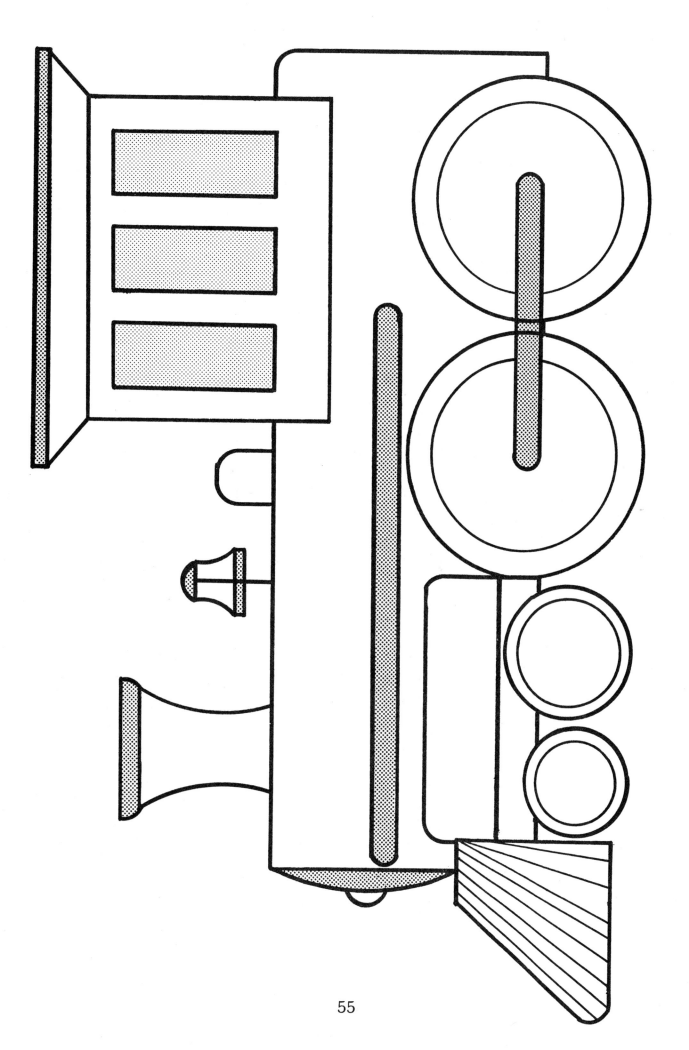

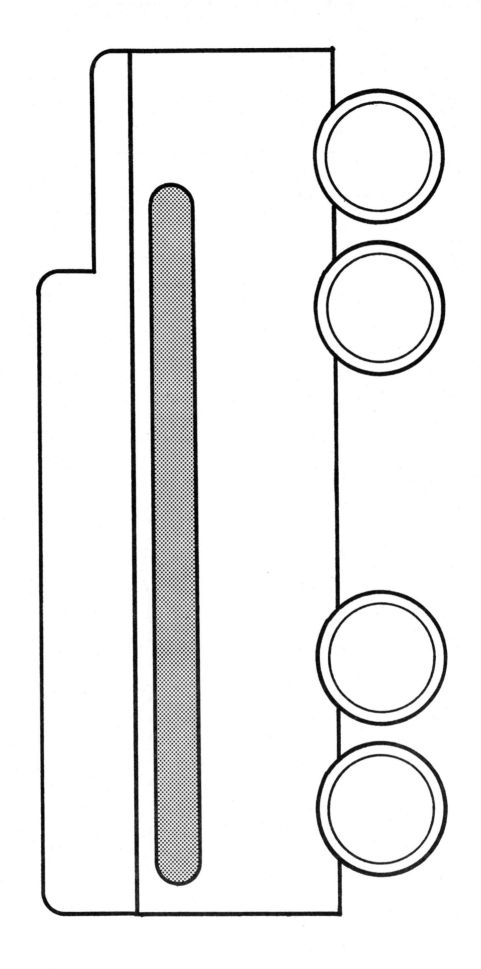

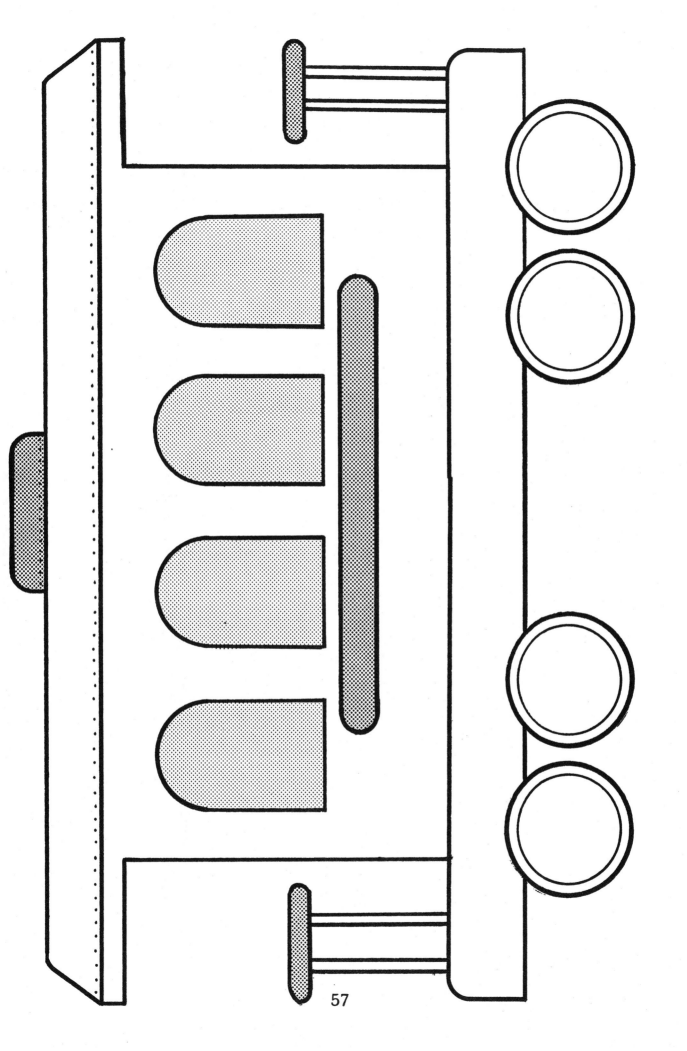

57

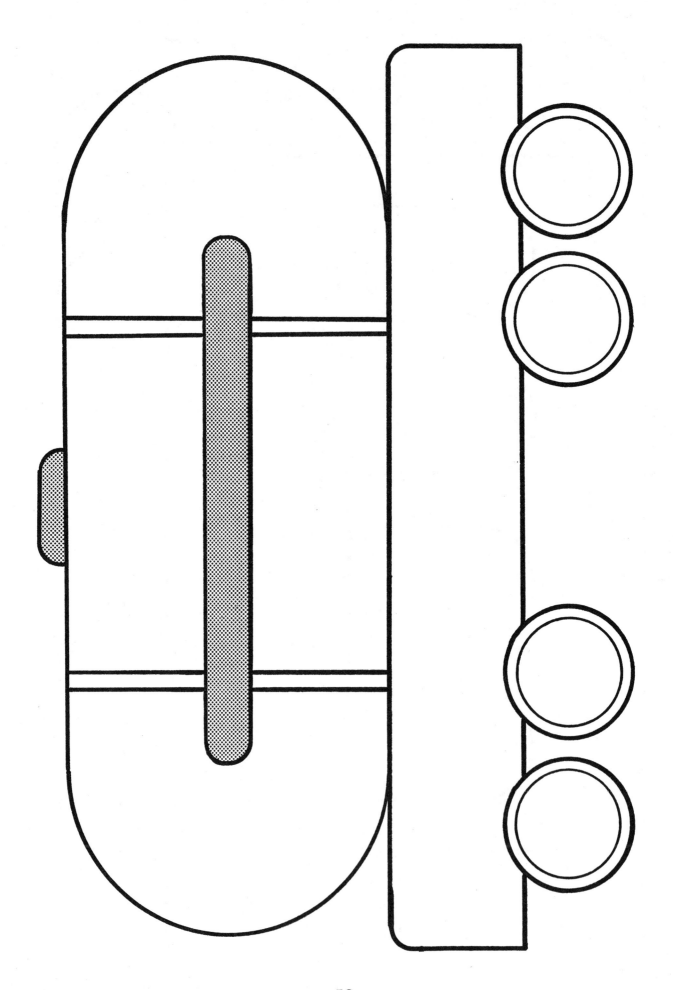

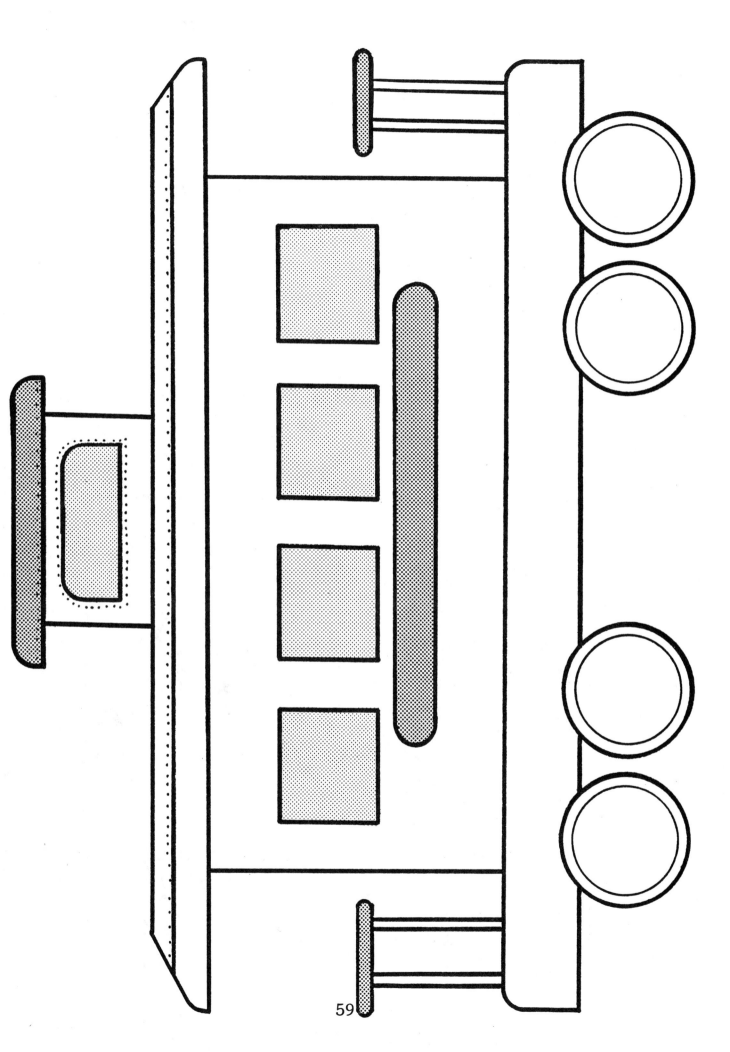

59

COLORFUL CATERPILLAR

Materials:
Butcher paper the size of your bulletin board
Heavy-duty wallpaper
Green construction paper

Activity: Cover the bulletin board with butcher paper. Make a large caterpillar face. Cut lots of large wallpaper circles for the caterpillar body. Keep them on an easily accessible shelf. Let the children fringe grass for the bottom of the board.

When the children finish artwork they would like to display on the caterpillar, have them get a wallpaper circle and bring it along with the artwork to you. Lay the art on top of the circle and attach it to the end of the caterpillar. The caterpillar may grow longer than your bulletin board so feel free to extend him onto the wall and around the room. (If you continue the caterpillar throughout the year he may wiggle all around your room. Oh! What a great display for a parent meeting!)

A child may want to take something off of one of his circles in the middle of the caterpillar. That's fine. The child may or may not have another piece he wants to display. If he does, help him hang it up. If not, simply leave the circle and let another child hang some art in that space.

60

ONGOING CREATIONS

"GETTING STARTED"

ONGOING CREATIONS DEVELOP WITH THE MONTHS, PROVIDING A BULLETIN BOARD DISPLAY WHICH CHANGES THROUGHOUT THE SCHOOL YEAR. INCLUDED IN THIS SECTION ARE 3 UNIQUE 'ONGOING CREATIONS'. CHOOSE THE ONE THAT IS MOST APPROPRIATE FOR YOUR CHILDREN AND THEN ENJOY WATCHING THE BULLETIN BOARD DEVELOP.

• "CRAYON CRAZINESS" FOCUSES ON COLOR COMPLIMENTED BY OPEN-ENDED ART ACTIVITIES FOR EACH MONTH OF THE SCHOOL YEAR.

• "GOING IN CIRCLES" USES 3 DIFFERENT SIZE CIRCLES. EACH MONTH THE CHILDREN WILL WORK WITH THE CIRCLES IN A DIFFERENT WAY. EACH MONTH THEY WILL USE A VARIETY OF MATERIALS TO RECYCLE THEIR CIRCLES INTO CHARACTERS, ANIMALS, AND OBJECTS.

• "OUR TREE" IS A BOARD WHICH WILL UNFOLD WITH THE SEASONS OF THE SCHOOL YEAR. THE TREE REMAINS THE FOCAL POINT OF THE BOARD, WHILE THE DETAILS CHANGE TO DEPICT THE LIFE ON AND AROUND THE TREE.

CRAYON CRAZINESS

Background: White butcher paper covered with brightly colored cookie cutter prints.

Main Component: Very large crayon shapes.

To Make: Before school begins cut white butcher paper to fit the bulletin board. During one of the first days of school have the children print the background paper using different cookie cutters and a wide variety of brightly colored tempera paint. Let the paint dry and hang the colorful background on the board.

Cut 9 very large crayons, one for each month of the school year, out of white posterboard or heavy white paper. Store them in an accessible place. Each month offer the children open-ended art activities to accent the featured color.

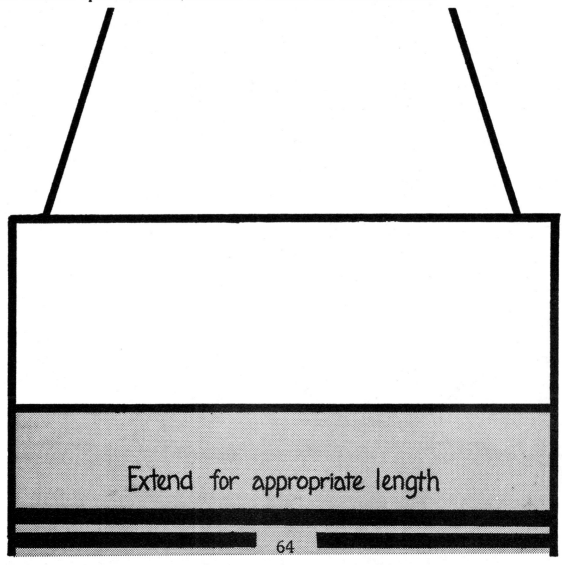

Extend for appropriate length

RED CRAYON

▐▬▌ Lay one of the white crayons on the art table and let the children use brushes to paint it with red tempera paint. When it is dry, hang it in the center of the bulletin board.

▐▬▌ During the month surround the red crayon with art the children do using red art materials. For example:
- Put 3 shades of red paint at the easel and let the children paint for several days.
- Cut apples into halves and quarters. Stick a fork into each piece for a handle. Let the children enjoy apple printing with red tempera paint on light colored construction paper.
- Have the children glue a variety of red papers on large scraps of red posterboard.
- Take a walk with the children. Have them collect fall leaves with red highlights. When you return to the classroom let the children glue the special leaves on paper.

▐▬▌ At the end of the month let the children take their red art home. Hang the tip of the red crayon under the bottom left-hand corner of the bulletin board.

YELLOW CRAYON

▐▬▌ Lay another white crayon on the art table. Have the children collage pieces of yellow tissue paper to the crayon. (Use liquid starch or watered-down white glue for the adhesive.) When the crayon is dry, hang it in the center of the board.

▐▬▌ During the month have the children hang their yellow art around the crayon. For example:
- Have the children use yellow chalk on white paper. When finished, spray their artwork with a fixative.
- Encourage the children to fingerpaint with yellow paint on fingerpaint paper.
- Have the children glue styrofoam bits on paper plates and paint their creations yellow.
- Cut a cleaned pumpkin into various small shapes. Using yellow paint, let the children pumpkin print on paper.

▐▬▌ At the end of the month, let the children take their yellow art home. Hang the yellow crayon to the right of the red one.

BLUE CRAYON

▐█▬▬█▶ Lay a large white crayon on the art table. Encourage the children to fingerpaint it with blue fingerpaint. Hang it on the bulletin board.

▐█▬▬█▶ During the month have the children hang their blue art around the blue crayon. For example:
   • Have the children cut different size blue circles, and collage onto light blue paper.
   • Using straws have the children blow dark blue paint over light blue paper.
   • Mix powdered blue tempera paint with each of the following: cornmeal, sand, and salt. Put the textured blue paint into 3 shakers. Have the children drizzle or brush glue on paper and shake the textured blue paints over their glue designs.
   • Invite the children to draw designs on white paper using a variety of shades of blue markers.

▐█▬▬█▶ At the end of the month let the children take their blue art home. Hang the blue crayon to the right of the yellow one.

GREEN CRAYON

▐█▬▬█▶ Have the children mix yellow and a little blue paint. Lay one of the white crayons on the art table and let the children sponge paint it with the green paint they just mixed.

▐█▬▬█▶ During the month have the children surround the green crayon with their green art. For example:
   • Put green, blue, and yellow tempera paint at the easel. Encourage the children to use the 3 colors and mix different shades of green as they paint.
   • Have the children use green paint and evergreen sprigs to color their paper.
   • Mix green food coloring with paste. Let the children enjoy fingerpainting with the colored paste on the shiny side of freezer wrap paper.
   • Put out a wide variety of green crayons. Encourage the children to draw pictures and designs on light green paper. When finished have them dictate a sentence or two about their drawings. Using green marker, write down what they say on green paper strips and attach them to their drawings.

▐█▬▬█▶ At the end of the month let the children take their green art home. Hang the green crayon to the right of the blue one.

WHITE CRAYON

▭▷ Have the children glue an assortment of white collage materials onto one of the white crayons. Hang it on the bulletin board.

▭▷ During the month have the children hang their white art around the white crayon. For example:
- Add texture such as salt or white sand to white tempera paint and let the children paint on colored paper.
- Have the children use white crayons to make designs on black construction paper and then brush over their drawings with watered-down white tempera paint.
- Gather different weights of white yarn. Cut them into varying lengths. Let the children glue yarn designs on white paper.
- Let the children collage a variety of white 3-dimensional objects such as cotton, styrofoam bits, bows, and paper cups onto white paper plates.

▭▷ At the end of the month send home all of the children's white art. Hang the white crayon to the right of the green one.

PINK CRAYON

▭▷ Lay one of the white crayons on the art table. Have the children string-paint it with pink paint. Let the crayon dry and then hang it on the bulletin board.

▭▷ Throughout the month encourage the children to hang their pink art around the pink crayon. For example:
- Let the children cut up different pieces of pink wallpaper and glue them to pink wrapping paper.
- Put red and white paint at the easel. Encourage the children to paint with both colors and see what happens.
- Using a variety of sizes of heart-shaped cookie cutters have the children print pink hearts on red paper.
- Cut pink sponges into a variety of shapes. Let the children sponge paint with pink paint on white paper.

▭▷ Have the children take their pink art home at the end of the month. Hang the pink crayon to the right of the white one.

ORANGE CRAYON

Lay one of the white crayons on the art table. Let the children color it using different shades of orange crayons. Hang it on the bulletin board.

During the month encourage the children to surround the orange crayon with the orange artwork. For example:
  • Let the children cut several shades of orange paper into strips and glue them onto orange construction paper.
  • Have the children make orange crayon shavings and then iron them between pieces of waxed paper.
  • Let the children make orange hand prints on paper. When they are finished, ask each child what he likes to do with his hands. Write down what he says on the bottom of his paper.
  • Use newspaper at the easel. Have the children use red and yellow paint and different width sponge brushes to paint their pictures.

At the end of the month have the children take their orange art home. Hang the orange crayon next to the pink one.

PURPLE CRAYON

Lay one of the white crayons on the art table. Have the children color it with purple chalk. Spray it with a fixative and hang it on the bulletin board.

Throughout the month encourage the children to tack their purple art to the bulletin board. For example:
  • Put different widths of purple markers on the table. Let the children draw purple designs on light colored purple construction paper.
  • Mix white and different amounts of purple to get several shades of purple paint. Have the children do eyedropper painting on purple paper.
  • Gather different items which have at least one circular side, such as corks, jar lids, spools, and cups. Have the children use these with purple, red and blue tempera paint to make circle prints.
  • Let the children enjoy dipping purple and white chalk into buttermilk and then drawing with the chalk on different types of paper.

At the end of the month have the children take all of their purple art home. Hang the purple crayon next to the orange one.

BROWN CRAYON

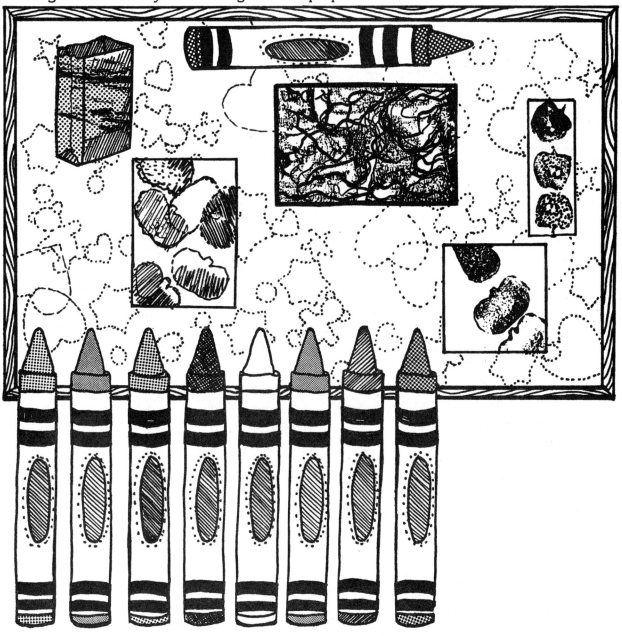

Lay the last white crayon on the art table. Encourage the children to paint it using brown tempera paint and feathers. Hang it on the bulletin board.

During the month have the children tack their brown art to the bulletin board. For example:

- Let the children paint large grocery bags with brown paint.
- Glue string designs using brown twine, ribbon, and yarn on brown paper.
- Put dried coffee grounds and/or tea leaf grounds into shakers. Let the children drizzle or brush glue designs on their papers and shake the grounds over them.
- Cut designs in potatoes and have the children do potato printing with brown paint.

When the month is over, give the children their brown art to take home. Hang the brown crayon to the right of the purple one.

GOING IN CIRCLES

Backgrounds: September, October, November—Gold background such as wallpaper.

December, January, February—Red background such as a bright wrapping paper.

March, April, May—Light green background such as shelf paper.

Main Component: Three different size posterboard circles.

To Make: Before school begins:
- Hang the gold background paper.
- Cut out a large (15″), medium (12″), and small (9″) circle from white posterboard.

70

APPLE FAMILY

Background: Gold paper

Border: Apple prints on 3″ or 4″ wide strips of white paper.

Main Activity: Have the children paint the 3 circles red, cut out a stem for each one, and glue the stems to the circles.

When the red paint is thoroughly dry, let the children paint a face on each of the apples and cut strips of red paper for the arms and legs. Staple the strips to the apple bodies. (Older children may want to fold the arms and legs accordion-style before stapling them to the bodies.) Tack the Apple Family to the board.
EXTENSION: Add other scenery the children would like such as colored leaves they have collected on a fall walk.

PUMPKIN PATCH

Background: Gold paper

Border: Remove the apple prints. Have the children make pumpkin cookie cutter prints on strips of white paper.

Main Activity: Remove the Apple Family from the bulletin board. Have the children carefully take the arms, legs, and stems off of the apples, turn the circles over, and paint the other sides orange. Add a stem to each pumpkin. Put the pumpkins on the bulletin board.

Using heavy yarn, string vines to connect the pumpkins. Tack the leaves which the children have painted or collected to the vines.

When it is closer to Halloween, you might want to have the children pick the pumpkins from the patch, change the pumpkins into jack-o-lanterns, and re-hang them on the board.

EXTENSION: Add a harvest moon and stars.

72

SCARECROWS

Background: Gold paper

Border: Continue to use the pumpkin print border from October.

Activity: Remove the jack-o-lanterns and vines from the board. Use the jack-o-lanterns as faces for the scarecrows. If the children did not change the pumpkins into jack-o-lanterns, have them paint scarecrow faces on the pumpkins.

Cut out 3 different size simple body shapes. Attach the appropriate size scarecrow head to each body. Have a collage box full of various fabric pieces and let the children glue patches to the scarecrow bodies. Hang the scarecrows on the board.
EXTENSION: Add crows flying around the scarecrows and a variety of vegetable prints showing off the fall harvest.

73

SHINING ORNAMENTS

Background: Remove the entire fall bulletin board. Tack up the red background paper.

Border: Scallop a garland and hang it around the edges of the board.

Activity: Remove the pumpkin stems from the 3 circles. Cover the circles with aluminum foil or foil wrapping paper. Let the children decorate the circles by gluing glitter, fabric trimmings, and wrapping paper scraps to them.

   Have the children make a hanger for each ornament by stringing 3 different lengths of paper chains and then attaching them to the top of each ornament. Hang the ornaments from the garland.
EXTENSION: Add artificial evergreen boughs in the corners.

SNOWMAN

Background: Red paper.

Border: Remove the garland. Using paper baking cups have the children cut out snowflakes. Hang them around the edges of the board.

Activity: Remove the 3 ornaments from the board and take off the aluminum foil. Using glue have the children cover the circles with white cotton balls.

Lay the circles on the art table from largest to smallest to form a snowman. Talk with the children about the snowman's features. (For example his face, buttons, hat, boots, broom, etc.) Using scraps from the collage box, have the children add the features they talked about.

When finished, tack the snowman to the bulletin board.

EXTENSION: Add more snowflakes cut from baking cups, a bright yellow sun, and some fluffy clouds.

SNOW-WOMAN

Background: Red paper.

Border: Keep the snowflakes around the edges of the board. Have the children cut out hearts or other designs and glue them onto the snowflakes.

Activity: Sit with the children in front of the bulletin board. Talk with them about how to change their snowman into a snow-woman.

The next day remove the snowman. Have all of the necessary supplies for the children, and let them change their snowman into a snow-woman. If some of the cotton balls fall off, have the children replace them. Hang her on the board.
EXTENSION: Add different colored hand print birds to use in February and March.

SPRING RABBIT

Background: Remove the entire winter bulletin board. Tack the light green background paper to the board.

Border: Glue colored cotton balls onto strips of paper and hang them around the edges of the board.

Activity: Carefully take all of the features off of each circle, leaving the cotton in place.

    Cut the medium size circle into 2 ear-shaped pieces. (See illustration.) Show the children how the largest circle will become the rabbit's body, the smallest size one his head, and 2 of the 3 pieces from the medium circle will be the rabbit's ears. (Save the third piece for April.) Talk about the features the rabbit needs.

    Have the materials ready the following day and let the children add the features to the rabbit. Give him a big fluffy tail.

EXTENSION: Add the colored birds you saved from February.

EASTER BUNNY

Background: Light green paper.

Border: Keep the cotton border from March around the 2 sides and the top. Fringe green paper grass for the bottom edge.

Activity: Keep the Spring rabbit on the board.

Cut a hat shape that is large enough to fit over the rabbit's ears. Have a collage box full of frilly fabrics, different bows, and ribbons. Let the children glue them onto the hat. When it is dry, tack the Easter bonnet to the bunny's head. Use the piece you saved from March for his fancy bow tie.

EXTENSION: Add a large basket filled with decorated paper eggs, and some blooming spring flowers poking through the grass.

SUN AND FLOWER

Background: Light green paper.

Border: Remove the cotton strips from the 3 sides of the board leaving the fringed green grass and flowers the children may have made.

Cut 3″ wide strips of white paper for the 2 sides and the top of the board. Have the children sponge paint yellow circles along the strips. When dry hang the strips up.

Activity: Remove the Easter bunny. Take off all of the bunny's features but once again leave the cotton on.

Put green, yellow, and a pastel color of dry tempera paint in three different salt shakers. Be sure that the shakers have small holes. Have the children shake the green paint on the two ovals, the pastel color on the smallest circle, and yellow on the largest circle. Jiggle the circles around a little, so that the paint settles into the cotton.

Use the pastel colored small circle for the flower with the 2 green ovals for the leaves. Add a stem. Hang the large yellow circle in the sky for the sun. EXTENSION: Have the children add petals to the central flower along with more spring flowers, butterflies, and clouds.

79

OUR TREE

Background: Light colored butcher paper.

Main Component: Tree with bare branches.

To Make: Tack the butcher paper to the board.
Make the tree in one of two ways:
• Using wide brown mailing paper draw a large tree shape to fit on your board. Cut it out and fasten it to the center of the board.
• Instead of cutting out a tree shape, use the brown mailing paper to form a 3-dimensional tree. Begin by cutting the paper into strips which are about 12 inches wide and 3 feet long. Twist each strip into a tight roll. Use 3 or 4 twisted strips bunched together to form the trunk and then curved out to form the main branches. Add shorter rolls if you want a fuller tree. Tack the tree to the center of the board.

Activity: Use this idea in August or the first part of September as a 'Welcome to School' board. Hang the children's and adults' name tags on the branches. When the children and adults come to school each day give them their name tags. They can put them on their shirts with tape or hang them around their necks. Near the end of the day put their name tags back on the tree.

FULL BLOOM
IN SEPTEMBER

Border: Remove the name tags from the tree. Tack them around the 2 sides and the top of the board. Have the children fringe strips of green construction paper for the grass. Staple this along the bottom edge of the board.

Activity: Have the children wad up pieces of light-weight brown paper into balls about the size of snowballs. Turn them into leaves for the tree by painting each ball with green tempera paint. After all of the balls have dried, tack them to the tree with thumb tacks or heavy-duty pins. You'll be removing the leaves in October to paint them again. EXTENSION: Add leaves, acorns, nuts, etc. that the children have collected on a fall walk.

FALL FOLIAGE
IN OCTOBER

Border: Remove the name tags and give them to the children to take home. You might suggest that they hang their name tags on their bedroom door knobs.

Cut 3″ or 4″ wide strips of white paper to fit around the top and 2 sides of the board. Using fall colors of paint, have the children make hand prints along the strips. When dry hang up the strips.

Activity: Carefully remove the green leaves which the children painted in September. Have the children change the green leaves into fall ones by painting them with bright fall colors. When the fall-colored leaves have dried, tack some of them to the tree and others on the ground.

EXTENSION: Add pumpkins which the children have painted. Towards the end of the month the children might want to change their pumpkins into jack-o-lanterns.

PREPARING FOR WINTER
IN NOVEMBER

Border: Keep the colored hand print border from October up until after Thanksgiving.

Activity: Remove the pumpkins and/or jack-o-lanterns.

Everyday have the children choose several leaves to fall from the tree to the ground. Tack the leaves to the ground.

After all of the leaves have fallen, let the children paint bird feeders to hang in the tree. You'll need white glue mixed with brown tempera paint and empty cream or whipping cream cartons.

Have the children paint the cartons with the brown glue and then sprinkle a little bird seed on each one. Let the feeders dry, punch a hole on 2 sides of each feeder, and string a piece of twine through each one. Hang the feeders in the tree.
EXTENSION: Add children's vegetable printings around the tree to celebrate the Thanksgiving Harvest. Older children might like to add birds, turkeys, Pilgrims, and Indians to the board.

LIGHTING UP THE SEASON
IN DECEMBER

Border: Remove the fall hand print border.

Using cotton batting, drape a blanket of snow over the fringed grass. Have the children string lights to go around the two sides and top of the board. (See 'Activity' below.)

Activity: Remove all of the fall art except the bird feeders.

Lay a long piece of brown twine on the art table. Have the children cut out circles from different colors of construction paper. Glue the circles along the twine. When dry hang the 'string of lights' on the tree.

EXTENSION: Add children's holiday art on each side of the tree. For example:

- Collage tissue paper scraps on small paper plates. Punch holes in the tops and string pieces of ribbon through them to make loops for hanging.
- Cut easel paper in large holiday shapes and let the children paint them.
- Add salt to your easel paint to give it a sparkling effect.

SNOWY DAYS
IN JANUARY

Border: Remove the string of lights from December.

Hang doily snowflakes around the top and sides of the board as well as over the blanket of snow. (See 'Activity' below.)

Activity: Remove all of the December art and the lights. Keep the bird feeders.

Have different size doilies. Let the children cut the doilies into different snowflake shapes. Hang the snowflakes on the tree and float them in the sky.
EXTENSION: Add different colored birds coming to the feeders. Older children might also want to include several hibernating animals such as the raccoon, snake, worm, woodchuck, skunk, and chipmunk.

SPRING'S IN THE AIR
IN FEBRUARY

Border: Keep the snowflakes around the edges. The children can cut out hearts to go in the center of each flake.

Activity: If the snow is gone in your area, remove the snowflakes from the tree and sky and the blanket of snow from the ground. Keep the grass beneath. If it is still snowing in your locale keep the snow on the board.

    With the children's help, combine Ivory Snow® and water to make textured white fingerpaint. Let the children make large billowy clouds for the sky by fingerpainting the mixture on fingerpaint paper. Let the art dry overnight. Trim the edges of the clouds and hang them in the sky.

EXTENSION: Add animals exchanging Valentines with each other.

SPRING FUN
IN MARCH

Border: Remove the hearts and any remaining snow. Keep the green fringed grass on the bottom edge.

Let the children make raindrop chains for the side and top borders.

Activity: Remove all of the bird feeders and any remaining snow.

Cut several kite shapes to fit in your tree. Have the children use straws to blow-paint different colors of tempera paint on the kites. Let them dry.

Attach a colorful piece of twine to each kite. Have the children make bows to put on the twine. Younger children might want to simply cut strips and glue them to the twine. Hang the kites in the tree.
EXTENSION: Add several gingerbread children dressed with collage materials flying kites.

THE TREE IS BUDDING
IN APRIL

Border: Remove the raindrop chains.

Put decorated paper eggs around the 2 sides and top border. (See 'Extension' activity below.)

Activity: Remove the kites from the tree.

Let the children make the spring buds for their tree by wadding up bits of green tissue paper and gluing them onto small pieces of green construction paper. Let the spring buds dry and then hang them on the tree branches.

EXTENSION: Add decorated paper eggs tucked in the grass and around the tree. Let the gingerbread children, who were flying kites in March, have an Easter egg hunt.

COMPLETELY GREEN
IN MAY

Border: Keep the decorated eggs. Take photographs of the children playing in different areas of the classroom and outside. Tack the photos in the centers of the eggs.

Activity: Cut a piece of brown mailing paper large enough to completely cover all of the branches of your tree. Lay it on the art table with green fingerpaint. Have the children fingerpaint the paper. Let it dry, round the edges, and then staple it over the branches.
EXTENSION: Add dandelions popping up in the grass, butterflies swooping through the air, and a big bright sun glowing in the sky.

TEACHER-MADE BOARDS

"GETTING STARTED"

TEACHER-MADE BOARDS HELP THE ROOM FUNCTION IN A MORE ORDERLY, CONGENIAL, AND INFORMATIVE ATMOSPHERE. THESE BOARDS ARE FUN TO USE WITH YOUR CHILDREN THROUGHOUT THE YEAR.

AS YOU'RE MAKING THE BOARDS TAKE FULL ADVANTAGE OF THE:

- EASY DIRECTIONS.
- PATTERNS WHICH CAN BE ENLARGED OR REDUCED.
- ACCOMPANYING ACTIVITIES.

WHEN USING THE BOARDS WITH YOUR CHILDREN:

- INVOLVE AS MANY OF THEM AS POSSIBLE.
- USE THE BOARDS REGULARLY TO DEVELOP A CONSISTENT ROUTINE.
- INCORPORATE CONCEPTS YOUR CHILDREN ARE LEARNING:
- EXTEND THE USE OF THE BOARDS ENJOYING ACTIVITIES THE CHILDREN SUGGEST.

OFF TO WORK WE GO

Materials:
Butcher paper to cover your bulletin board
Piece of posterboard
8 large sheets of different colored construction paper
Wooden spring-loaded clothespins
Wide-tipped markers
Fine-tipped markers
Old magazines
Heavy-duty twine or yarn

To Make: Make a list of the 6 to 8 jobs around the room that you want the children to be responsible for. Cut a large circle out of posterboard. Divide it into 6 to 8 equal triangles. Cut the colored construction paper to fit on the posterboard triangles. Glue them to the posterboard. In each triangle glue a magazine picture (or one you have drawn) to represent the job you want done.

Print the children's names on the clothespins. Hang a piece of twine or yarn from the ceiling near the job wheel and clip the clothespins to it.

To Use: Talk with the children about all of the jobs they will be responsible for. Show them the clothespins with their names on them. Tell them that when it is their turn to do a particular job you will clip their clothespin to that job section on the wheel. When you change the jobs talk with the children about their new jobs. For example if Miles will be passing out the napkins, clip his clothespin to the section of the job wheel with the napkins pictured on it. This will remind Miles what his job is when he looks at the wheel. Children who are not currently responsible for a job will have their clothespins attached to the string.

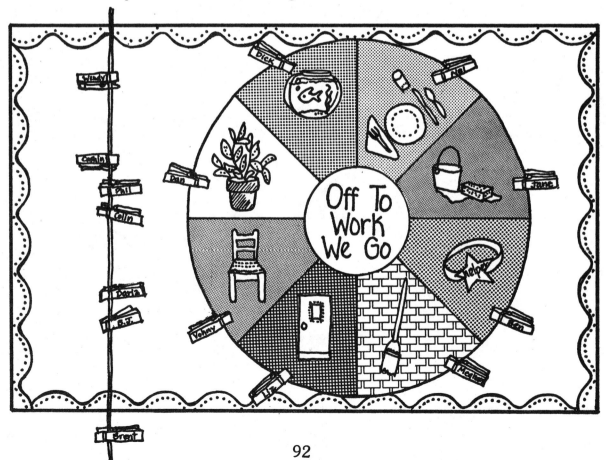

CHILD OF THE WEEK

Materials:
Black background paper to cover the board
White construction paper circles
White strip of posterboard to fit along the bottom of the board

To Make: Tack the background paper to the board. Cut 15 to 20 large white circles to represent lights. Tack them along the top of the board. Using the red marker print the name of the child who is being featured that week in the lights. On the posterboard strip which fits along the bottom of the board, print "Coming Next Week." On a strip of construction paper print the name of the child who will be featured the following week. Tack the name on the far right of the posterboard strip.

To Use: Have a folder for each child. From the very beginning of the year begin collecting art work, photos, and other memorabilia pertinent to each child. Put the pieces in the folders. Have the child bring in 'things' he would like to display on the board during his week.

At the beginning of the week take out the featured child's folder. Show him what you have collected. Look at what he has brought from home. Let him choose what he would like to hang on the board and where he would like it hung. Tack it all up.
EXTENSION: Each day have the featured child choose one activity he would like to do that day. For example:

Monday, he chooses a favorite book for you to read.
Tuesday, he decides what colors of paint will be at the easel.
Wednesday, he names a fingerplay or song he wants everyone to sing.
Thursday, he can bring in a stuffed animal he would like to tell the class about.
Friday, he can lead the group when going out of the room.

HAPPY BIRTHDAY

Materials:
Butcher paper or birthday wrapping paper to cover your bulletin board
Large cake shape cut out of posterboard
Large construction paper or posterboard birthday candles
Wide marker
Cereal box
Medium size gift box with a lid
Birthday wrapping paper
Birthday crowns and badges cut out of posterboard or heavy paper

To Make: Decorate the birthday cake and print "Happy Birthday" on it. Hang it in the center of your bulletin board. Cover the cereal box and print "Birthday Candles" on it. Hang the candle box on the board. For each child who has a birthday in the month, print his age on a candle and his name on the candle holder. Place all of the month's birthday candles in the candle box.

Decorate the gift box with birthday wrapping paper and attach it firmly to the board. On each child's birthday put a birthday crown and badge in the birthday gift box.

To Use: Celebrate each child's birthday at circle time. Begin by taking his birthday candle out of the box, giving it to him, and helping him put it on the cake. Sing "Happy Birthday" to him. Have him make a wish and pretend to blow out the candle. Let him choose a song or fingerplay he likes and then lead the group in it. Let him name a game which he likes. Play it. After the game have him go over to the birthday box and get his special crown and badge. He can decorate them at the art table after circle time and then wear them for the rest of the day.

When he goes home give him a birthday hug and make certain he has his crown, badge, and birthday candle.
EXTENSION: You might want to give each child in your class a simple birthday present such as a small book, a box of crayons, bubbles and wand, or a cup of soft dough that you have made along with a cookie cutter of his age. You could include the gift in the birthday box.

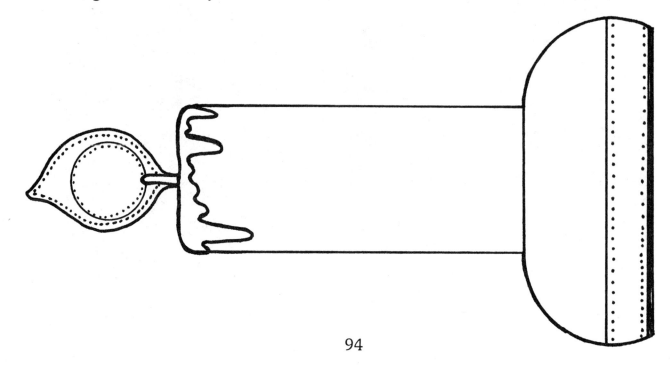

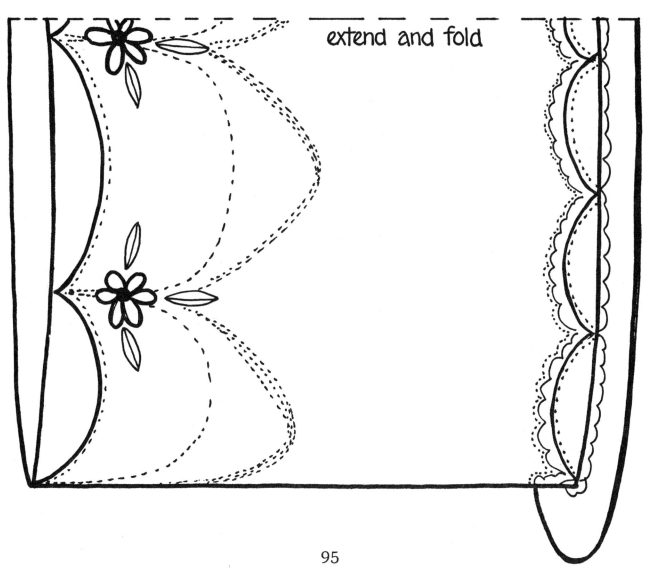

extend and fold

COUNTDOWN CALENDARS

Materials:
Butcher paper to cover your bulletin board
Long strip of paper from 3" to 6" wide
Construction paper
Wide-tipped marker

To Make: Decide what up-coming event you and the children are looking forward to, such as a holiday, a field trip, chick's hatching, a special visitor, parents' day at school, and so on. Using construction paper make a large symbol representing the event, maybe a heart for Valentine's Day, a pumpkin for a trip to the pumpkin farm, etc.

Using construction paper, cut small countdown symbols with a child's name on each one, to use on the calendar strip. This symbol could be the same as or different than the large one. For example you could use Valentine cards, a school bus, and so on.

Tack the large symbol near the bottom of your bulletin board. Cut the strip so it reaches from the top of your board to the symbol. Write number 1 at the bottom of the strip and continue numbering up until you've written one number for each child in the class. Tack the strip to the bulletin board with the number 1 just above the large symbol. Tack each child's symbol to the left/right of the countdown calendar.

To Use: The appropriate number of days before the event, introduce the countdown calendar to the children. Talk about the large symbol and what will happen on the special day. Let one child cover the top number with his countdown symbol.

Each day have a different child cover the next number. As the trail gets closer to the symbol, the children will realize that the event is getting closer. The number 1 should get covered the day before the event.

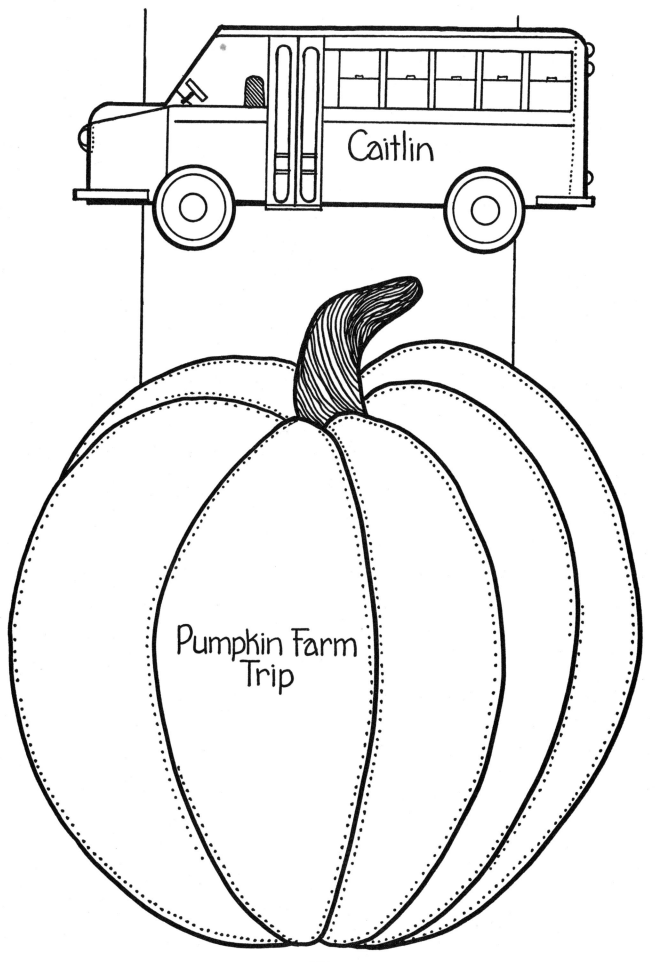

Caitlin

Pumpkin Farm
Trip

97

Daniel

Valentine Exchange

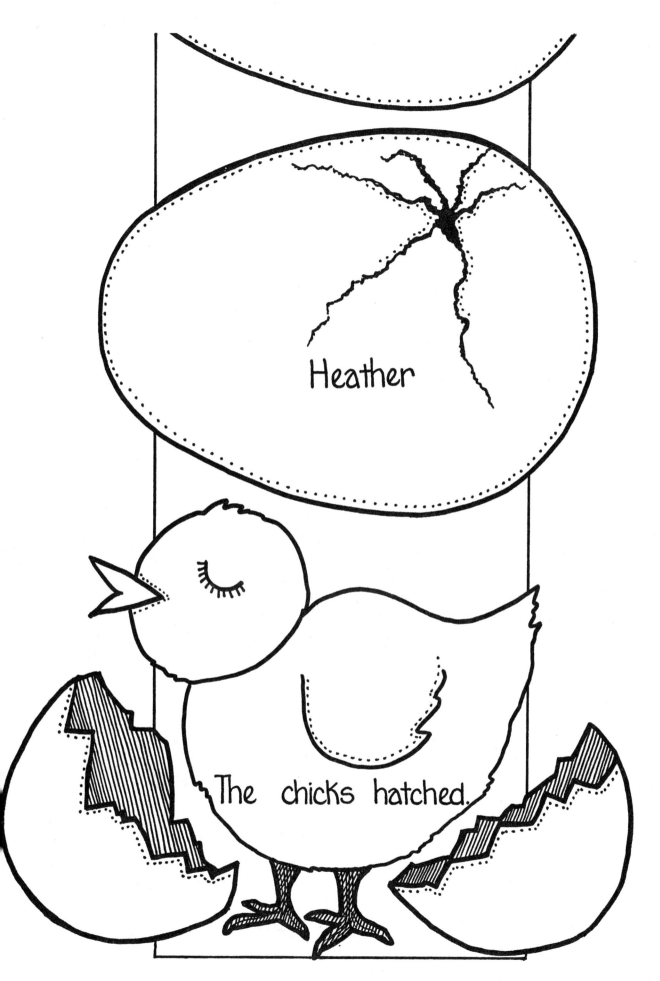

WEATHER REPORT

Materials:
Butcher paper to cover your bulletin board
Large white pizza board or posterboard circle
Several spring-loaded wooden clothespins
Fine-tipped markers
Wide-tipped markers
Felt child and clothes appropriate for different types of weather
Several pairs of binoculars made out of two toilet paper rolls glued together
File folder

To Make: Make a list of the types of weather that are common in your area. Count them and then, using a wide marker, divide your circle into that many equal sized sections. In each section draw a simple picture (or use copies of the enclosed illustrations) of one of the types of weather. Hang the weather wheel on the board.
　　Print "Today is" on several clothespins.
　　Fasten the felt child next to the weather wheel.
　　Make a suitcase for the felt child's clothes by cutting out 2 construction paper handles and gluing them to the top edges of the file folder.
　　Cut out the felt clothing and put the pieces in the suitcase.
　　Hang the binoculars on a low hook near the weather wheel.

To Use: Ask a child to get a pair of binoculars, walk over to a window, look out and describe the weather outside. Ask another child to get a pair of binoculars, join the first child and add anything else about the weather.
　　Now have several children take the clothespins and find the pictures on the weather circle which correspond to the children's descriptions. Clip the clothespins to the circle.
　　You can also discuss the types of clothes people wear in the particular type of weather. Have the children find the appropriate clothes in the suitcase and then dress the felt child.

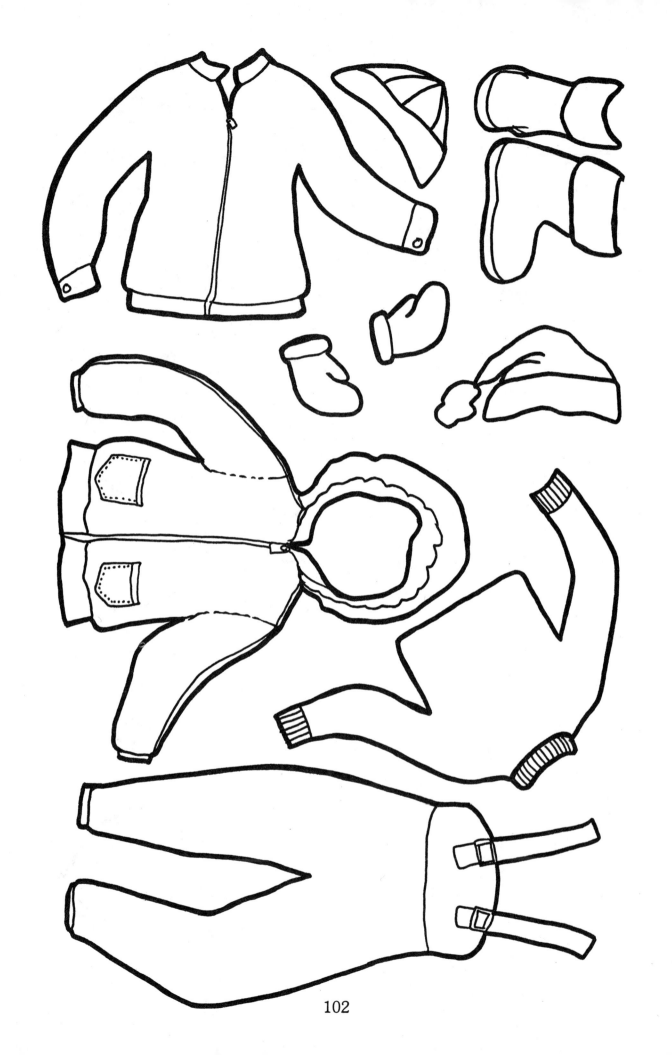

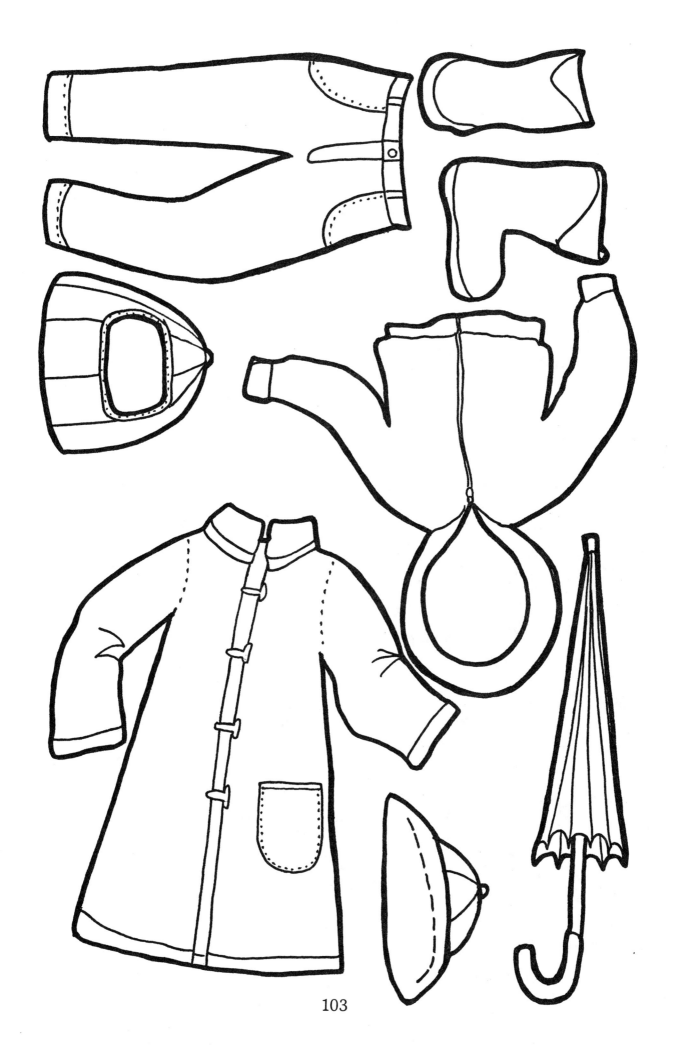

Sunny

Partly Sunny

Cloudy

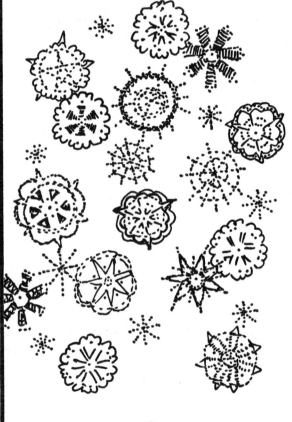

Snowy

Rainy

Windy

Stormy

Foggy

OCTO SAYS, "KEEP IN TOUCH"

Materials:
Butcher paper to cover your bulletin board
Piece of posterboard
Strips of butcher, wall, or shelf paper
Construction paper

To Make: Cut the posterboard into a large circle and draw an octopus face on it. Tack the face to the middle of your bulletin board. Cut 8 tennacles out of the strips of paper. Tack them around his head. Along each tennacle tack a piece of construction paper. These will be the backings or frames for your parent announcements, monthly menus, health news, calendars, and so on. From construction paper, cut out Octo's hats. (See patterns.) Put one on him. Add a border if you want.

To Use: At the beginning of each month (or when appropriate) remove the old news. Change the colors of the construction paper frames to symbolize that month. Tack up the current announcements. Your parents may have announcements to share with each other. Have a space for them to tack up their news. Change Octo's hat and border when appropriate.

Encourage your parents to read the announcements on the board when they drop off and pick up their children.

107

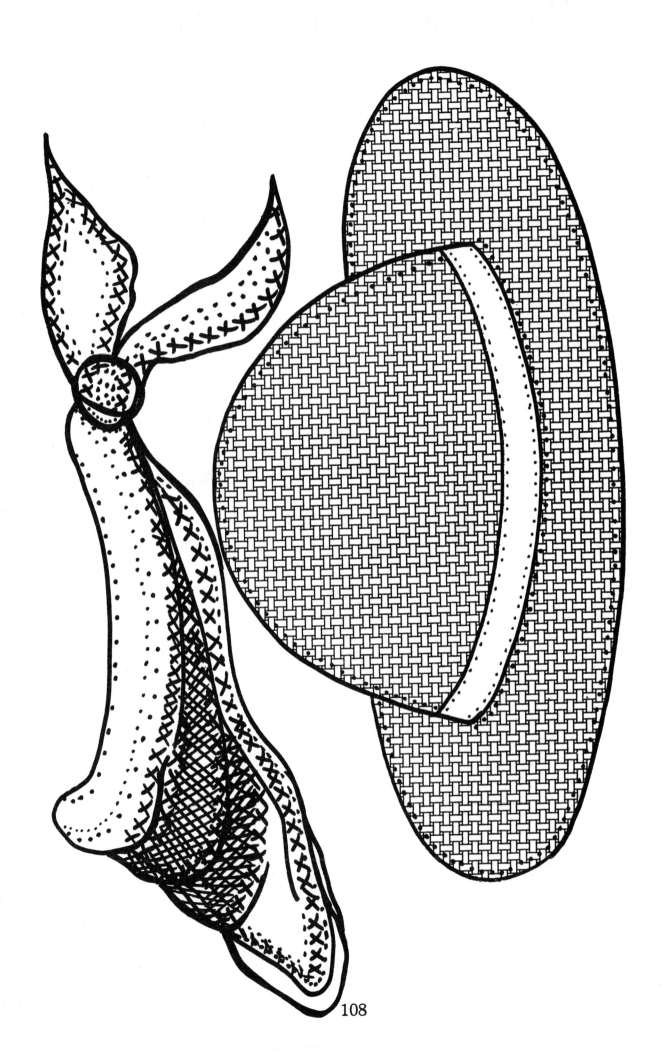

108

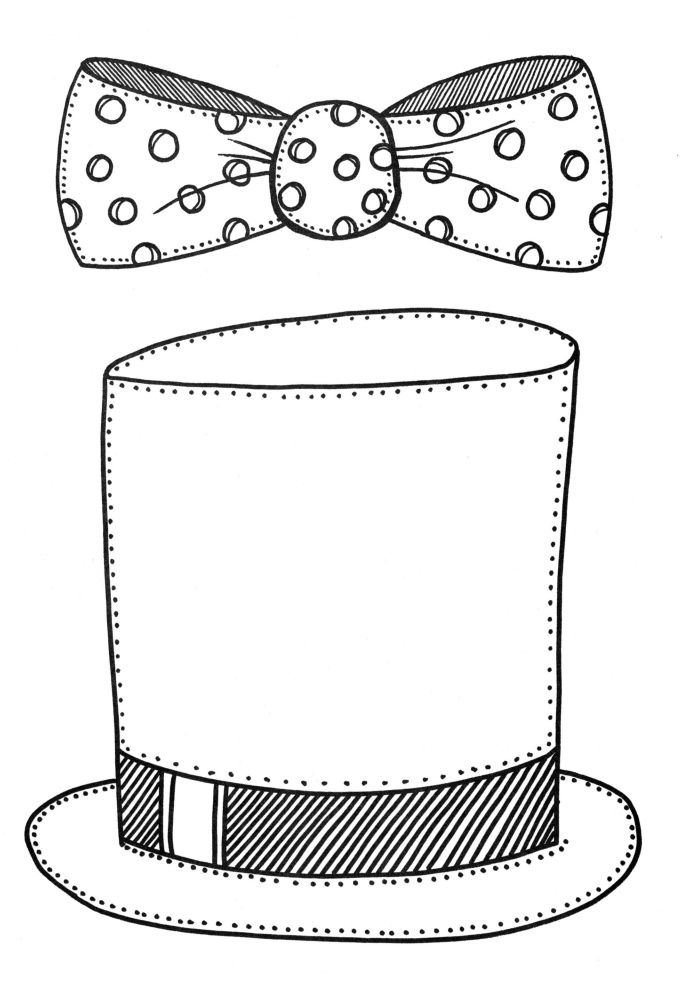

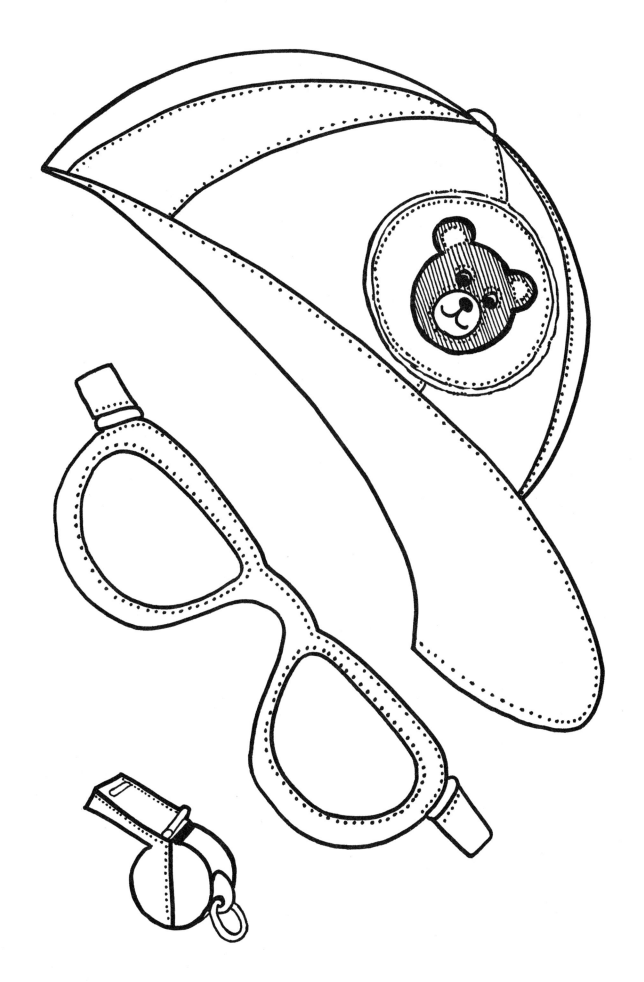

APPENDIX

More Borders

Artificial flowers

Banners
Bows

Cartoon strips
Commercial borders
Container lids
Coupons
Crepe paper streamers

Doilies

Envelopes

Food box covers
Food labels

Garlands
Gauze
Greeting Cards

Leaves
Lunch bags

Magazine pictures
Mittens
Muffin cups

Neck Ties

Paper chains
Photographs
Play money
Postcards

Register tape

Small paper plates

Wide ribbons

More Backgrounds

Aluminum foil

Beach towels
Book covers
Bubble plastic
Butcher paper

Cereal boxes (cut them open)
Computer paper
Colored corrugated paper
Construction paper

Doilies

Fabrics
Fish net

Greeting cards

Large posters

Mailing paper
Maps

Newspaper
Newsprint end rolls

Paper tablecloths
Paper towels

Shelf paper
Shower curtain

Tissue paper

Wallpaper
Wrapping paper

Buildng Blocks Library

The Circle Time Series

by Liz and Dick Wilmes. Hundreds of activities for large and small groups of children. Each book is filled with Language and Active games, Fingerplays, Songs, Stories, Snacks, and more. A great resource for every library shelf.

Circle Time Book
Captures the spirit of 39 holidays and seasons.
ISBN 0-943452-00-7 **$ 9.95**

Everyday Circle Times
Over 900 ideas. Choose from 48 topics divided into 7 sections: self-concept, basic concepts, animals, foods, science, occupations, and recreation.
ISBN 0-943452-01-5 **$14.95**

More Everyday Circle Times
Divided into the same 7 sections as EVERYDAY. Features new topics such as Birds and Pizza, plus all new ideas for some familiar topics contained in EVERYDAY.
ISBN 0-943452-14-7 **$14.95**

Yearful of Circle Times
52 different topics to use weekly, by seasons, or mixed throughout the year. New Friends, Signs of Fall, Snowfolk Fun, and much more.
ISBN 0-943452-10-4 **$14.95**

Paint Without Brushes

by Liz and Dick Wilmes. Use common materials which you already have. Discover the painting possibilities in your classroom! PAINT WITHOUT BRUSHES gives your children open-ended art activities to explore paint in lots of creative ways. A valuable art resource. One you'll want to use daily.
ISBN 0-943452-15-5 **$12.95**

Gifts, Cards, and Wraps

by Wilmes and Zavodsky. Help the children sparkle with the excitement of gift giving. Filled with thoughtful gifts, unique wraps, and special cards which the children can make and give. They're sure to bring smiles.
ISBN 0-943452-06-6 **$ 7.95**

Everyday Bulletin Boards

by Wilmes and Moehling. Features borders, murals, backgrounds, and other open-ended art to display on your bulletin boards. Plus board ideas with patterns, which teachers can make and use to enhance their curriculum.
ISBN 0-943452-09-0 **$ 8.95**

Exploring Art

by Liz and Dick Wilmes. EXPLORING ART is divided by months. Over 250 art ideas for paint, chalk, doughs, scissors, and more. Easy to set-up in your classroom.
ISBN 0-943452-05-8 **$16.95**

C I R C L E   T I M E

A R T

ASSORTED

LEARNING GAMES

Parachute Play

by Liz and Dick Wilmes. A year 'round approach to one of the most versatile pieces of large muscle equipment. Starting with basic techniques, PARACHUTE PLAY provides over 100 activities to use with your parachute.
ISBN 0-943452-03-1   **$ 7.95**

Classroom Parties

by Susan Spaete. Each party plan suggests decorations, trimmings, and snacks which the children can easily make to set a festive mood. Choose from games, songs, art activities, stories, and related experiences which will add to the spirit and fun.
ISBN 0-943452-07-4   **$ 8.95**

Imagination Stretchers

by Liz and Dick Wilmes. Perfect for whole language. Over 400 conversation starters for creative discussions, simple lists, and beginning dictation and writing.
ISBN 0-943452-04-X   **$ 6.95**

Parent Programs and Open Houses

by Susan Spaete. Filled with a wide variety of year 'round presentations, pre-registration ideas, open houses, and end-of-the-year gatherings. All involve the children from the planning stages through the programs.
ISBN 0-943452-08-2   **$ 9.95**

Learning Centers

by Liz and Dick Wilmes. Hundreds of open-ended activities to quickly involve and excite your children. You'll use it every time you plan and whenever you need a quick, additional activity. A must for every teacher's bookshelf.
ISBN 0-943452-13-9   **$16.95**

Felt Board Fun

by Liz and Dick Wilmes. Make your felt board come alive. Discover how versatile it is as the children become involved with a wide range of activities. This unique book has over 150 ideas with accompanying patterns.
ISBN 0-943452-02-3   **$14.95**

Table & Floor Games

by Liz and Dick Wilmes. 32 easy-to-make, fun-to-play table/floor games with accompanying patterns ready to trace or photocopy. Teach beginning concepts such as matching, counting, colors, alphabet recognition, sorting and so on.
ISBN 0-943452-16-3   **$16.95**

Activities Unlimited

by Adler, Caton, and Cleveland. Create an enthusiasm for learning! Hundreds of innovative activities to help your children develop fine and gross motor skills, increase their language, become self-reliant, and play cooperatively. Whether you're a beginning teacher or a veteran, this book will quickly become one of your favorites.
ISBN 0-943452-17-1   **$16.95**

2'S Experience Series

by Liz and Dick Wilmes. An exciting series developed especially for toddlers and twos!

2's Experience - Felt Board Fun
Make your felt board come alive. Enjoy stories, activities, and rhymes developed just for very young children. Hundreds of extra large patterns feature teddy bears, birthdays, farm animals, and much, much more.
ISBN0-943452-19-8   **$12.95**

2's Experience - Fingerplays
A wonderful collection of easy fingerplays with accompanying games and large FINGERPLAY CARDS. Put each CARD together so that your children can look at the picture on one side, while you look at the words and actions on the other. Build a CARD file to use everyday.
ISBN 0-943452-18-X   **$9.95**

Watch for more titles in the 2's Experience series.

All books available from teacher stores, school supply catalogs or directly from:

Thank you for your order.

38W567 Brindlewood
Elgin, Illinois   60123
800-233-2448   708-742-1054 (FAX)

Name_____

Address _____

City_____

State_____ Zip _____

QUALITY
BUILDING BLOCKS
SINCE 1977

	Each	Total
BUILDING BLOCKS Subscription	20.00	_____
2's EXPERIENCE Series		
2'S EXPERIENCE FELTBOARD FUN	12.95	_____
2'S EXPERIENCE FINGERPLAYS	9.95	_____
CIRCLE TIME Series		
CIRCLE TIME BOOK	9.95	_____
EVERYDAY CIRCLE TIMES	14.95	_____
MORE EVERYDAY CIRCLE TIMES	14.95	_____
YEARFUL OF CIRCLE TIMES	14.95	_____
ART		
PAINT WITHOUT BRUSHES	12.95	_____
EXPLORING ART	16.95	_____
EVERYDAY BULLETIN BOARDS	8.95	_____
GIFTS, CARDS, AND WRAPS	7.95	_____
LEARNING GAMES		
ACTIVITIES UNLIMITED	16.95	_____
FELT BOARD FUN	14.95	_____
TABLE & FLOOR GAMES	16.95	_____
LEARNING CENTERS	16.95	_____
ASSORTED TITLES		
CLASSROOM PARTIES	8.95	_____
IMAGINATION STRETCHERS	6.95	_____
PARACHUTE PLAY	7.95	_____
PARENT PROGRAMS/OPEN HOUSE	9.95	_____
	TOTAL	_____